UNDERSTANDING SCHNAUZERS

The German noun Schnauze means snout or muzzle. The name Schnauzer, therefore, calls attention to the characteristic squarish, whisker-fringed mouth of this charming and robust breed of dog.

History of the Breed

Pictures of dogs painted as early as the fifteenth century depict Schnauzers, which can be recognized by their body and head shape, prominent eyebrows, and silver-brindle-colored wiry coat. These dogs are the ancestors of the modern Standard Schnauzer.

Three distinct Schnauzer breeds, differing in body size, are recognized by the American Kennel Club: Miniature, Standard, and Giant. (See pages 90–91 for size, range, and weight for each breed.)

Most experts believe that the Miniature Schnauzer is the result of crossbreeding Poodles and Affenpinschers with smaller Standard Schnauzers. If this is correct, the addition of these other two breeds with their positive traits of vigor and intelligence certainly

The Standard Schnauzer is the oldest of the three Schnauzer breeds.

improved the result. According to the American Kennel Club, the Miniature Schnauzer was first recognized as a distinctive breed as early as 1899. Miniature Schnauzers have been bred in the United States since 1925, and the American Miniature Schnauzer Club was chartered as an independent breed organization in 1933. Although Schnauzers have steadily gained in popularity, they nevertheless have largely escaped the deterioration that so many popular breeds have suffered through indiscriminate breeding. Schnauzer breeders have carefully selected breeding stock and have wisely avoided the sale of lesser-quality pups. In many other dog breeds, genetic defects have been allowed to accumulate and thereby lower the quality and vigor of the puppies.

Statistics for the year 2000 furnished by the American Kennel Club reveal that the Miniature Schnauzer ranked 16th among the 140 breeds enumerated. The Giant Schnauzer ranked 77th, the Standard Schnauzer 100th, in breed preference or popularity.

Although some older dog books list all the Schnauzers as guard dogs, the American Kennel Club considers the Miniature Schnauzer to be a terrier; in general, the physical characteristics and temperament are consistent with those of terriers. Miniature Schnauzers physically resemble other terriers bred in Britain during the last two or three centuries to serve as ratters—small dogs combining the traits of intelligence, strength, and valor, able and willing to attack rodents in their labyrinthine lairs. The Miniature Schnauzer, while possessing these traits, is, however, a remarkably sociable and human-oriented creature.

The Nature of the Schnauzer

Perhaps the very best adjective to describe Schnauzers of any size if *feisty*. Like most, if not all, terriers, Schnauzers also display a wonderful enthusiasm and *joie de vivre*. They are usually quite gentle with resident household children, yet make modest-sized, adequate watchdogs. While not going out of its way to pick a fight, a typical Schnauzer usually will not retreat from an aggressive encounter and is quite capable of giving a good account of itself. Since my wife and I were married in 1956, we have shared our home with many dogs. Without question, our best watchdog was an 11-pound Miniature Schnauzer. More than once we watched in awe as that small dog confronted and refused to back away from a head-to-head challenge by adult Hereford cattle!

Physically, the Giant Schnauzer measures 25½ to 27½ inches (64.8–69.9 cm) at the shoulder and weighs from 80 to 110 pounds (36.4–50 kg); the Standard Schnauzer measures 23 to 25 inches (58–64 cm) and weighs from 45 to 60 pounds (20–27 kg); the Miniature Schnauzer measures 12 to 14 inches (30–36 cm) and should weigh from 9 to 16 pounds (4–7 kg). Generally males will be larger than females. When fully mature, all Schnauzers are robust and sturdy animals.

Typically, the coat of these dogs consists of two types of hair: the outer wiry guard hair and an undercoat of fine, soft, and silky hair. The coat color may range from light or dark silver-gray, to finely mottled brindle, to almost black. The individual hairs are banded with light and dark areas that impart the familiar "salt and pepper" or brindled color effects.

Characteristic Behavior Patterns

Vocal Communications

Standard Schnauzers possess a voice typically associated with a large dog, full of authority and capable of commanding the immediate attention of household residents in case invited or uninvited persons arrive. Being intelligent dogs, they can be trained not to bark incessantly. Schnauzers, like so many of the terrier-type breeds, tend to be more apt to bark, especially at the approach of strangers and other dogs.

Depending upon the circumstances, other vocalizations can be barks of joy at seeing favored family members returning from an absence; yelps of pain, or calls to entice someone to play; howls at the sound of an emergency vehicle's siren; growls at intruders, or at

Get to know the facial expressions of your Schnauzer and you should be able to read its moods.

play, such as tugs-of-war with a toy; and (particularly in puppies) miscellaneous whines and whimpers. Most commonly, Miniature Schnauzers confine their vocalizations to sharp barks.

Body Language

Dogs can effectively communicate with each other and with people by stereotyped body language.

Tail wagging is one of the most recognizable non-vocal communications, but the manner in which the tail is carried also indicates the emotional state of dogs. A tail carried at a jaunty angle, or wagging slightly like a waving flag is a sure sign of canine contentment. A lowered tail that is tucked between the rear legs is a certain signal that the dog either is in the immediate presence of what it considers a dominant creature or is cowering in wary expectation of punishment. Even those Schnauzers whose tails have been surgically docked can convey their emotions by the way they wag their abbreviated tails. Some dogs will actually smile by drawing back their lips as they wag their tails with exuberance; others smile with their tails alone!

The carriage of the ears also conveys nonvocal messages of how a dog feels at any given moment—though, in a Schnauzer with cropped ears, the ear flaps (or pinnae) are much less mobile than those of an individual with natural, uncropped ear flaps. When content or while investigating something within their domain, Schnauzers tend to carry their ears erect with only the outer third bent forward by

their own weight. When unhappy, fearful, or ill, Schnauzers tend to allow their ears to droop against the top and sides of the head.

If sufficiently long, the hairs on the top of the neck and just in front of the root of the tail become erect when the dog becomes agitated. It is thought that this behavior is a remnant of prehistoric times when confrontations were much more common. The heightened silhouette makes each of the potential combatants appear larger than life, and thus more formidable.

When happy, Schnauzers often "dance" about on their feet, especially their front feet, in an obvious display of bliss at being noticed.

Facial Expressions

When content, the facial expression of the Schnauzer reflects interest in its surroundings. At first sign of anything novel, the ears are immediately elevated and the eyes scan intently for visual clues. The nasal openings flare in an attempt to detect unfamiliar scents.

When stirred to aggression, the lips may be curled, exposing the teeth, particularly the

The Miniature Schnauzer is equally comfortable in town or country.

A healthy curiosity is an essential part of puppyhood.

incisors and canines. Without a peaceful resolution of the situation, the lips are then drawn further and the mouth is held open, fully exposing the teeth and tongue, which is curled and held away from the incisors. The ears are carried in a flattened position. Given the opportunity, the dog may either attack or withdraw from the confrontation. If the situation is not relieved and escape is impossible, the mouth is opened further, the growls become louder and more forceful, and the ears point forward toward the object of aggression.

The bushy eyebrows, so characteristic of the breed, also add to the Schnauzer's nonvocal expression; just prior to attacking, the brows become furrowed. This imparts a squint to the eyes.

Fortunately, Schnauzers generally are not especially aggressive, and only resort to this behavior when severely provoked or are acting to protect their human family's territory and possessions.

Scent Marking

Schnauzers, like all other breeds of dogs, "stake out" their territory by scent marking fixed objects along their perceived boundaries. This is accomplished in two ways: urine is deposited onto surfaces such as trees and shrubbery, and anal scent is deposited onto formed stools as they pass through the anus. The anal scent is secreted by paired, bean-shaped glandular sacs situated at openings into the anal canal at the four o'clock and eight o'clock positions. Occasionally, these sacs become impacted with the dried secretions. The affected dog "scoots" on the ground in an effort to relieve the discomfort caused by the inflamed sacs. (See page 83.)

While it is normal for a Schnauzer to scent mark its territory, if that territory is within your dwelling, that behavior must be modified and redirected to a more suitable area outdoors. Often this can be accomplished by walking your dog on a leash so that it can establish its own territory in the neighborhood. Of course, your Schnauzer may have to share its new territory with other dogs, but that only reinforces each dog's zeal to mark objects—with the result being that the bladder and anal sacs are more completely emptied. As each vertical or horizontal "signpost" is encountered, the dog will sniff it to find out what messages have been left since his or her last visit. A tail wag signals a friendly "note"; a growl indicates an unfriendly "letter."

Considerations of Social Dominance

When you share your home with but a single Schnauzer, it is common for the dog to consider itself submissive to its human owner. When more than one dog is in the family, it is normal for one of the dogs to assert its dominance over the other. Very submissive dogs will exhibit their deference by rolling over on their side or back and releasing a variable amount of urine. This is a signal to the dominant animal that it is primary—in other words, that an attack is unnecessary. The act of

Schnauzer puppies grow at an amazingly rapid rate.

rolling over and urinating in the presence of their owners is also exhibited by insecure dogs, particularly when any effort is made to pick up the dog or to discipline it. To an aggressor dog, the message is clear. To humans, the message is interpreted as only another mess to clean up. With confidence gained as a consequence of the owner's patience and *consistent* correction of misbehavior, most dogs will outgrow this trait swiftly.

The Sense Organs

Of the five senses that Schnauzers share with their human friends, scent, hearing, and taste appear to be superior. Some hunting breeds, such as the Greyhound, Whippet, Saluki, and Afghan Hound, possess excellent sight; they have been bred for centuries to chase very fast prey such as hares. Schnauzers, having been bred as ratters, rely upon very keen senses of smell and hearing. Since taste is so closely related to smell, it is not surprising that the sense of taste appears to be more acute in the canine than in humans. Only touch is more highly developed in humans than in dogs, but dogs do not need to rely on the tactile sense in their everyday dealing with this environment.

From Puppy to Adult Dog

From the time of birth to weaning, at about five to six weeks, the Schnauzer puppy changes quite a bit, but not as much as from weaning to young adulthood. The newborn multiplies its bulk four- to fivefold during the first six weeks, as its muscles, skeleton, internal organs, and coat grow at a tremendous rate. The caloric intake in proportion to body weight during this critical growth period exceeds that of the mature dog, which needs only to maintain its weight. (The nutritional requirements for your Schnauzer puppy will be discussed in the chapter on nutrition. See pages 45–51.)

Socialization, or the adaptation of a puppy to human beings in the absence of the puppy's mother, begins as early as seven weeks of age and appears to be complete around ten weeks of age. For this reason a puppy should be obtained around the seventh week of life. At this age it will transfer its allegiance to humans rather than to dominant dogs, as would be the case with a normally pack-socialized animal. Beyond the 10–12-week period, the human-dog social bonding is less readily achieved. For this reason some young dogs raised from puppyhood to adulthood with little or no close contact with humans make unsatisfactory companion animals.

Female puppies achieve early sexual maturity at five to seven months of age. This range is variable, just as it is in humans. Males tend to attain their sexual maturity several months later, and most are capable of becoming fathers by the time they are 10 to 12 months old. By the time of early puberty, male Schnauzers (sometimes also females) will begin to lift one leg when they urinate. Interestingly, dogs tend to favor one leg over the other.

Schnauzers of both sexes continue to grow slowly and "fill out" until they are well into their second year of life. Many will retain their puppylike behavior into middle age; some continue to enjoy playing like adolescent youngsters even when they are past ten years of age. This is another very positive and delightful trait of the breed.

Middle age for most Miniature Schnauzers occurs around 9 to 11 years. The onset of middle age for Standard Schnauzers is usually a year or two earlier, and for the Giant Schnauzer often as early as 7 years. During this time, some slight dullness might be noted in its eyes. This mild clouding of the crystalline lenses of the eyes is a normal consequence of aging and usually does not substantially lessen eyesight. As the dog ages, its lenses may become progressively opaque, but this is usually a very gradual process with which most aged dogs can readily cope. As the dog reaches late middle age, at about 12 years, its' hearing may become less acute, just as its owner's hearing does at an equivalent biological age. Again, this is a gradual function of aging and usually is of little consequence.

Just as in humans, aging also carries with it a greater incidence of arthritis, heart disease, dental problems, diabetes, and tumors. As your Schnauzer grows old, regular health-maintenance examinations by your trusted veterinarian will help ensure a long and satisfactory life for your loved pet. Dogs of all breeds are now enjoying longer and healthier lives because of advances in veterinary medicine.

Contact with the World and Other Dogs

It is vitally important to bond with your Schnauzer. Also, it is essential that your dog *knows* that it is a dog, not a short four-legged human wearing a fur coat. Schnauzers, like other breeds, should have contact with other dogs so they can learn to relate to nonhuman beings when encountered outside of home territory.

Once it is properly immunized against infectious diseases, even a young puppy should be taken outdoors to learn about the world. A leash and a training collar that will not injure its tender neck will make these learning experiences more comfortable for all concerned. Moreover, the puppy will begin its early obedience training during its youth by becoming accustomed to wearing a collar and being led on a leash. Simple commands are learned at this time. By the time the puppy is half-grown, it should have already mastered those manners that make any dog a positive part of your life.

This looks like the start of a long, happy relationship.

Behavioral Disturbances

Like humans, some dogs develop psychological abnormalities, which in their complexity, often mimic similar disturbances in humans. Some breeds appear to carry a genetic predisposition for some of these behavioral traits. Fortunately the Standard and Miniature Schnauzers seem free of these genetically linked disturbances, and if they are intelligently trained and cared for, they make excellent companion dogs for young and old alike. Many animal observers note that Schnauzers may, like other dog breeds, exhibit special fondness for one member of the family over the rest, but it is almost unheard of for the dog to display open aggression toward a household resident. In those very rare instances when this occurs, it can almost always be traced to mistreatment of the dog by that person. Happily, the Giant, Standard, and Miniature Schnauzer are not inherently vicious breeds whose militant protective instincts are easily released.

CONSIDERATIONS BEFORE YOU BUY

With the population of the United States moving from mainly single-family housing to multifamily housing, the smaller breeds of dogs are becoming more attractive as companion pets.

Is a Schnauzer the Right Dog for You?

Many of the physical traits of the Miniature Schnauzer make it particularly suitable for today's (and tomorrow's) housing situations. It is a compact, sturdy breed with a coat that requires minimal grooming. Its fur is not particularly prone to excessive shedding—as long as nutrition is satisfactory and the skin remains healthy. The breed is prized for its native intelligence and loving personality.

By now you should have checked your lease to make sure that it allows you to keep a dog in the rented apartment or house. If the landlord's permission is required, obtain it in writing.

For the best opportunity to evaluate Schnauzers, attend one or more dog shows to compare

Be sure you can be happy with a Schnauzer before commencing the search for your perfect pet.

the characteristics of the breeds you see. Talk to dog breeders, handlers, and judges and seek their counsel. Everyone has prejudices and preferences concerning favored dog breeds, but at least you will obtain a cross section of opinions.

Giant, Standard, or Miniature?

To many, the three versions of Schnauzers are equally suitable for companion dogs. Often the size of housing determines which size of dog to adopt. If part of the decision rests upon the prospective dog's role as a watchdog, the Giant or Standard Schnauzer can back up its bark with more than enough authority. However, the Miniature Schnauzer's voice and ability to protect its (and your) territory is often quite sufficient. Anyone familiar with the breed will not doubt its courage and tenacity.

The Miniature Schnauzer is small enough to allow it to be picked up, as necessary, whereas the Giant and Standard Schnauzers are an armload for a strong man. The Miniature is unlikely to upset its owner while being walked on a leash if it suddenly bolts at the sight of some distraction, like a running cat or squirrel. Of course, the smaller dog eats less, eliminates a smaller volume of urine and feces, is much easier to bathe and groom, and requires much less space for its sleeping quarters. Automobile trips are far less crowded with the Miniature, and vacationing with a small dog is far less trying than with a much larger canine. While some hotels and motels allow their guests to register with small dogs, many are unwilling to accept large dogs. For those who spend much of their time aboard boats or in recreational vehicles, the smaller breed is a sensible choice. By the way, most Schnauzers of any size appear to enjoy water.

While not invariably the case, Miniature Schnauzers tend to live longer lives than their larger relatives. When everything is considered, the smaller dog will cost much less than the Giant or Standard Schnauzer.

A happy and attentive young Schnauzer.

A Puppy or a Mature Dog?

While it is a delight to watch a dog grow from puppyhood to adulthood under your guidance, it also requires much effort and time on your part. The young puppy is a "clean slate" with respect to its treasury of learned behavior. Any habits that your new dog develops will be acquired while it is in your care.

The older dog, when it first enters your home, will bring with it both positive and negative habits. The likelihood is that behavioral disturbances that had been fixed in an older dog will remain lifelong, no matter how hard you work to correct them. The mature dog may not have socialized properly during its critical seven- to ten-week teachable period. Another drawback of adopting a mature dog is that some adult dogs find it very difficult to adjust to new surroundings after being raised elsewhere.

For these reasons I recommend that Schnauzers be obtained as puppies.

Male or Female?

There are many misconceptions about which sex of dog makes the best companion pet. Either sex will become an affectionate and very suitable pet, because it is the manner in which it is treated by you and others in your household that determines the dog's response to humans. One cannot demonstrate that males or females offer advantages over one another.

Male dogs tend to grow to a somewhat larger size than females. Adult male dogs are more persistent than females in scent marking their territories, though both will display this behavior to some extent. If a male Schnauzer detects the scent of a female in heat, he will react to that nearly irresistible stimulus by trying to reach the source of that scent cue; a simple screen door is no barrier when primal urges are inflamed. Sexually aroused male dogs may display habits which, while entirely normal, are considered socially unacceptable in polite company. Unless you definitely plan to employ your male Schnauzer as a stud dog, there are some compelling reasons to have him neutered just before he is one year old. This subject is discussed at length on page 74; suffice it to state here that with proper care, nutrition, and exercise, the neutered male dog lives a longer, more healthy life than he would if he had not been surgically altered. Neutered dogs, of course, do not develop tumors or other diseases of the testicle or prostate, nor are they likely later in life to develop perineal hernias or perianal gland tumors.

Females usually come into their first estrus at about the age of seven months. This onset of sexual maturity may be slightly earlier or may be delayed by a month or two. Schnauzers, being fastidious creatures, usually keep themselves clean, but some discharge may stain carpeting or upholstery. Protective devices that look like infants' panties and are fitted with a pocket into which a cotton gauze pad is inserted can be used to prevent both soilage and accidental breeding by an attentive male. Chlorophyll-containing tablets available from veterinarians also will, if administered *before the onset* of a heat period, greatly diminish the sexually attractive female scent.

Just as with male Schnauzers, unless you wish to mate your female and raise her puppies, she should be spayed before her very first heat period. There are many myths about this subject. Some hold that all female puppies should be allowed to either experience one or two estrus cycles or bear at least one litter of puppies before being spayed. Common sense and actual physiological studies agree that this is poor advice. As a veterinary surgeon, I can see no valid reason to allow a female to achieve full sexual maturity and then reverse the process and induce future potentially serious ovarian hormone-deficiency effects afterward. My own formal research in comparative cancer pathology and research by my colleagues here and abroad have conclusively shown that spaying a female before her very first estrus tremendously reduces the probability of breast cancer later in life. Even those few breast tumors that may develop in a small number of spayed females are usually benign and not life-threatening. Of course, diseases of the ovaries and uterus and many disorders affecting the vagina are prevented by the ovariohysterectomy (spay) operation.

The comparative prices for male and female Giant, Standard, or Miniature Schnauzers are so close that price alone should not determine which sex to choose.

Where to Obtain a Schnauzer Puppy

There is an ancient saying that if you ask two wise men a question, expect three answers. Perhaps this is the case with respect to where to seek your Schnauzer. The choices are professional breeders, amateur breeders who may have but a single female and contract for stud service, and pet shops.

Like anybody else, I have my prejudices and firmly believe that you will most readily find an excellent dog and in the long run save a substantial amount of money by obtaining

your new dog from a breeder. More often than not, there is a warranty for the health and soundness of a Schnauzer purchased from a breeder. Responsible breeders certify that all their brood females are properly vaccinated and dewormed before being bred. A wealth of sound information on your new puppy and what to feed it and how to groom it is most likely going to be available from a breeder specializing in Schnauzers.

The nicest dilemma the pet owner will face is picking the right puppy.

Reliable pet shops obtain their stock from reliable breeders. Some pet shops, on the other hand, purchase their stock from so-called "backyard" breeders. Because of their high turnover of puppies obtained from a variety of sources, often without a quarantine, these pet shops tend to accumulate a population of varied infectious bacterial, viral, and parasitic diseases that may thus be readily transmitted to unvaccinated and/or worm-infested puppies in such an environment.

Anyone who decides to buy a Schnauzer from a pet shop should ask the pet shop owner for the name, address, and phone number of the dog's breeder.

What Traits to Look For in Selecting a Puppy

It is strange but true that many people, if given the opportunity to choose from a wide variety of very similar animals, will pick the smallest, most feeble, wretched, or even deformed individual from a litter, flock, herd, or school. Without commenting on *why* some people specifically pick the runt of a litter of puppies, I will offer some suggestions on how to intelligently select a strong and sound puppy that will grow into an adult dog with whom you will be sharing many happy and healthful years.

Take your new puppy to a nearby veterinarian as soon as possible. If the puppy has any diagnosed health problems, notify the seller immediately.

Your Schnauzer will incur a certain amount of maintenance cost over the course of its lifetime. If you are like most dog owners, you will consider that cost small, compared to the pleasure you will get from your special companion.

Because dogs are pack animals and begin their canine socialization during their nursing time while being cared for by their dam and while roughhousing with their littermates, one should specifically look for a lively, alert, even mildly aggressive puppy who is playing an active role in the litter. It should be responsive to gentle handling and possess a clean, moist nose pad, bright inquisitive eyes, and have reasonable coordination in his movements.

The myth that only healthy dogs have cold, wet nose pads is just that—a bit of lore, repeated from generation to generation. It is important that the nostrils be free of mucous

exudate, as should the eyelids. There must be no hint of coughing. The coat should be clean and free from any wastes or mucus. Most young puppies have little pot bellies, but they should not be excessively distended. The mouth and oral cavity should be examined to ensure that the hard palate is intact and that there are not gross abnormalities.

In summary, the new puppy should be full of life and intense interest in its surroundings and in you as its potential new owner and companion.

The Age of the Puppy at the Time of Selection

Puppies should be fully weaned by the time they reach six and a half weeks of age. Even before they are taken away from their dam, they probably have been nibbling upon commercial dry food, cottage cheese, unflavored yogurt, and drinking skim or cultured butter-milk. In my opinion, the ideal age at which to select and introduce a puppy to its new home is seven weeks.

When it reaches eight weeks of age, the puppy should receive its first immunization injection against the major infectious diseases and should have been treated for infestation with roundworms. Even the cleanest and best-operated kennels cannot totally rid their stock of the common roundworms, because these parasites spend a portion of their life cycles outside of the gastrointestinal tracts of the females. During late pregnancy, some of these worm larvae cross the placental membranes through which the developing puppy fetuses are nourished. Within a few weeks, these worms migrate through the tissues of the pup-pies and eventually reach the stomach and intestines, where they mature. For this reason your veterinarian will ask you to submit a fresh stool specimen from your puppy on its first well-puppy visit. It is an excellent practice to bring your new pup to the family veterinarian soon after you obtain it; the fee is wisely spent because, if any major defects are revealed, the puppy needs to be returned to the breeder for a replacement or refund. If you wait too long, you will lose this consumer right for financial compensation.

How to Choose a Mature Schnauzer

If your desire for a mature Schnauzer and the opportunity to obtain one coincide, there are some guidelines that will help you select a dog who will make a splendid companion for several years.

Whether Giants, Standards, or Miniatures, adult Schnauzers often can be adopted into your family. In contrast to selecting a young puppy in which early development of coordina-tion and juvenile behavior are all-important, one places more emphasis upon the personality of the adult dog. If you note that the prospec-tive adult Schnauzer tends to cower or is openly aggressive with strangers, you may be sure that the dog is demonstrating signs of psychological disturbances that probably will make it unsuitable as a companion.

A dog with obvious diseases or disorders should be avoided. Remember that once you have accepted the new dog into your family, your attachment will grow stronger with the passage of time; it will be much more difficult to separate yourself from the dog than it would be to reject it from the very beginning.

Prior to obtaining it, the dog should be examined by your veterinarian to certify that your choice is sound.

Must the Tail Be Docked and Ears Be Cropped?

For many years it was fashionable for owners of many breeds of dogs to have their animals' tails cut short. Similarly, some breeds had their ordinarily long ear flaps shortened and trimmed so that they would stand erect. For humane reasons these practices have fortu-nately fallen into disfavor by many veterinari-ans. This author also is one of those disapproving the practice. The British Veteri-nary Medical Association has been in the fore-front of those professional groups discouraging their members from this mutilation of perfectly healthy organs. In the United States, some

Schnauzers with uncropped ears are just as handsome as cropped animals.

states have declared it unlawful to perform these "cosmetic" operations, especially when they involve the ears. A valid case, however, *can* be made for tail docking in those breeds with especially long and powerful tails, and in instances of injury to the tail. Many people find that a Schnauzer with a natural-length tail looks as good or better than one whose tail has been docked short.

The individual breed clubs sanctioned by the American Kennel Club are now becoming enlightened in not rejecting show dogs whose tails and/or ears are natural. Also, dog show judges have become accustomed to judging dogs on the merits of their positive natural qualities and are ignoring the artificiality of surgically altered ears; for this they are to be applauded.

Costs of Purchase and Maintenance

Although the selling prices of high-quality Giant, Standard, and Miniature Schnauzers vary widely across the United States, some averages can be calculated by comparing newspaper advertisements from various locales. In early 2001, a companion-grade Standard Schnauzer puppy cost between $375 and $500. Of course, some exceptional animals command higher prices. A companion-grade Miniature Schnauzer costs from $175 to $350. A Giant Schnauzer costs from $350 to over $600, depending upon its quality. These figures depend on the quality of the dog, and they vary geographically. Very fine show stock

would cost twice this amount but, with the increased popularity of the breed and the larger number of puppies being produced, the price is descending slowly.

Veterinary fees for routine multi-injection vaccinations and deworming, obedience training equipment, doggy utensils, and bedding designed for the Giant, Standard, and Miniature Schnauzers will amount to another $225 to $375, depending on your geographical location and the nature of veterinary practice. In those regions where heartworms are prevalent, prophylactic anti-heartworm medication will cost about $45 to $90, depending upon the size and weight of your Schnauzer and the brand of drug administered. Food costs vary widely with the products fed and the amount fed, but will probably add an additional $60 to $115 for the first year. Some of the wholesale warehouses sell several of their own brands and excellent national brands at substantial savings. Purchase enough to last six to eight weeks. After the package has been opened, place the food in a tightly closed vermin-proof container, stored in a cool, dry place.

SUPPLIES AND HOUSING

Besides a nutritious diet, dogs must always have ready access to clean, fresh water in a suitable bowl.

Availability of Fresh Water

Domestic dogs prefer to drink from standing water several times during the day. If they are fed dry food, their consumption of water will be correspondingly greater than if they are fed moist or semimoist diets. In nature, wild (feral) dogs tend to drink less often, but lap up a greater volume at one time.

Water may be offered in a broad-based, wide-mouthed container, or from a ball-check automatic sipper device that attaches to water pipes outdoors. If a bowl is furnished, it must be cleaned regularly. Saliva and standing water provide a ready home to bacteria and fungi that can infect your dog.

Proper Toys

Although they are not essential to a dog's intellectual development, playthings such as

The Giant Schnauzer benefits from ample living space to suit its energy and exercise requirements. Obviously Standard and Miniature versions will not need the Giant's amount of "elbow room."

balls and bonelike objects are enjoyed by almost any dog. Schnauzers, being curious creatures always exploring their environment, soon choose those toys that are of particular interest to them.

Balls should be made from nontoxic materials and should be sufficiently sturdy to survive frequent mauling. It is very important that all toys be large enough to prevent their being accidentally swallowed or choked upon.

Rawhide bones or the hard-milled nylon bones appear to be well accepted by even the most eager Schnauzer who is teething. Large beef knuckle bones obtained from your butcher may be prized by your Schnauzer, but after your carpeting, upholstery, clothing, and dog have become messy with tallow and bone marrow remnants, you will rue the day you gazed into those two expressive brown eyes and allowed your Schnauzer to gnaw on a real bone.

Chicken, turkey, lamb, pork, or smaller beef bones also should be avoided because they may splinter and injure delicate soft tissues after they are swallowed by your dog.

Pieces of rags, nylon hose, pantyhose, and similar stringy objects and materials must be

CHECKLIST

Grooming Supplies

✔ Slicker brush or soft-bristle brush
✔ Metal comb
✔ Canine shampoo
✔ Natural or cellulose sponge
✔ Cotton balls
✔ Bland petrolatum-based ophthalmic ointment
✔ Gentle spray hose or plastic pan for rinsing
✔ Bathtub with nonskid surface or rubber mat insert
✔ Towels
✔ Nail/claw clippers

avoided, because they are readily swallowed and can produce serious, even fatal, damage to the tender gastrointestinal tracts of young dogs. Similarly, old shoes, belts, and other objects of apparel should not be offered as toys, because adornments and laces may become detached and swallowed, necessitating surgical intervention. Some materials are toxic and others will block the passage of food and stools through the gastrointestinal tract.

Stuffed toys with sewn-on eyes and the like are unsafe for dogs because they may be easily gnawed, pulled off, and swallowed, thus causing choking and/or intestinal obstruction. Similarly, if your Schnauzer puppy is sharing its new home with a baby, you must be careful not to allow the puppy to have access to nursing bottles and especially rubber nipples, for they can be accidentally swallowed and cause much trouble.

Sleeping and Feeding Areas in the House

Dogs, like their human companions, have definite preferences for sites where they rest and sleep. For a minority of dogs, their owner's bed is their preferred "nesting" place and they both share the blankets. In some instances, this arrangement can be defended, but generally the dog should have its own bed. If for no other reason, hygienic considerations should rule out shared human-canine sleeping quarters. Certainly the cleaning bills will be far less if the dog is not allowed to use its owner's bed.

Our own Schnauzer chose one of two comfortable leather-upholstered chairs for her bed. Most pet shops carry or can order wicker baskets that have been designed as dog beds. A form-fitted mattress with a washable cloth cover is placed into the basket. Most Schnauzers will accept this arrangement as their own in a very short time.

It is very important that whatever you use for your dog's sleeping quarters be situated in a draft-free place that is readily accessible to both you and your Schnauzer. Young puppies should be carried to their new bed each time you find them sleeping in some other place. Schnauzers are intelligent and will soon learn that only the bed you provide is the proper place to sleep.

If at all possible, a small, freely swinging "doggie door" should be installed, so that your pet can go outside to eliminate whenever it wishes to do so. Obviously, this arrangement is impossible in a high-rise apartment or condominium, but it is very desirable in a ground-floor home.

An Outdoor Run?

An outdoor run is often constructed for housing and exercising some dogs, especially those of larger size. If manicured gardens must be kept dog-free or if your living style does not permit regular leash-led walking exercise, an outdoor run might be considered. The Miniature Schnauzer, being a modest-sized dog, generally does not warrant an outdoor run. Moreover, Schnauzers are very human-oriented, sensitive creatures and, if given the opportunity to be polled, probably would eagerly choose closer contact with their owners than is afforded by a kennel and outdoor-run environment.

If an outdoor run must be used, it should have a sloping concrete surface that can be readily washed down daily. There must be provision for the disposal of feces without creating a vermin hazard. Many commercial kennels employ heavy-duty garbage disposal units plumbed into the sewerage line for this purpose. The walls of the run area should be constructed from chain-link fencing so that your dog can, at the very least, see some of its surrounding world. Remember, no housing arrangement for an animal must be so sterile that boredom will lead to behavioral disturbances. Many professional dog handlers have observed that dogs kept in kennels generally are not as social as those allowed to live in the home environment with their owners.

A doghouse or rain-tight, draft-free shelter should be provided so that your dog will have a comfortable place in which to retire and/or seek refuge from the elements. If a doghouse is planned, it should be designed with an airspace between its floor and the concrete surface. The floor of the house should be fitted with durable padded carpeting. The doghouse should have a removable roof so that the interior of the shelter can be cleaned routinely. To prevent drafts, the doorway should be provided with a piece of heavy carpeting or similar material, hung from above. Some shade-providing overhang or foliage also should be present.

A ready source of fresh drinking water is an absolute necessity. Automatic self-actuated drinking devices are available from animal feed dealers and some pet shops. These low-pressure drinking fountains are ideal for kenneled dogs because they cannot be fouled with food or wastes. In freezing weather, they can become inoperative if the water pipe is left exposed.

Some consideration must be given to the potential noise and odor pollution that an outdoor-kenneled dog can generate. Even the best-mannered canine will bark from time to time, and your neighbors' rights to peace and quiet must be respected.

In order to eliminate unpleasant odors and fly infestation, your dog's stools must be disposed of frequently and properly. An outdoor run can be maintained in a socially acceptable fashion, but it takes some effort.

KEEPING AND CARING FOR SCHNAUZERS

Having recently been separated from its mother and siblings, your new puppy will need your understanding and forbearance for the first few weeks after being introduced into the unfamiliar environment of your home.

Helping Your Puppy Get Started

The puppy is a naturally curious canine, very eager to examine and sniff everything that is new to it. During this same time, its new teeth are just beginning to push through the gums, and the desire to gnaw nearly everything within its new world often provokes the new owner.

One of the very first things that you should do is to show your Schnauzer puppy where it can find its food and water. Select a site in your kitchen or utility room where it is convenient for you to place the food and water. Most healthy puppies have ravenous appetites and you can use this to your advantage. At least for the first week

Learn how your Schnauzer responds to its environment and you can shape its personality to suit your needs in a wonderful pet.

or two, feed your puppy the same food that was being offered at the kennel. Later, if you wish to change the diet, do it gradually over a period of a week or two, starting with 90% original food and 10% new food, increasing the percentage of new food daily until the entire diet is composed of the new item(s). Once your puppy becomes accustomed to receiving its food from you, the gradual process of the human-animal bond and socialization will be well on its way.

The two qualities that are needed to train a dog are *firmness* and *consistency*. If you are going to assume your proper role as the dominant individual in the human-animal bonding process, you must establish that your commands must be obeyed. If you corrected the pup for a misdeed yesterday, you *must* use the same correction for that same infraction today and tomorrow. Nothing will confuse a young dog more than uncertainty about your reaction to its behavior.

Here is a practical example. What should you do when the new puppy whines when left alone in its bed at the time you retire for the evening? This whining is perfectly normal, because before entering your home, the puppy had its mother and littermates to comfort it and keep it occupied. You should go back to the basket, pet the puppy as you speak to it in soothing tones, but *do not* pick it up or allow it to follow you back to your bedroom. If your resolve wilts at this "moment of truth," your future relationship with your dog will surely be confused.

Never leave a young puppy alone in your home during the first few days after acquiring it. Remember, this is a critical time in the bonding and early training process, and you must avoid allowing the puppy to feel it is being abandoned. If this happens, the puppy will probably take out its frustrations by first giving in to the urge to incessantly whine and bark. When this behavior fails to bring you back, the puppy will usually begin to chew on any object in its grasp. The damage to your home during even a brief absence can be substantial, and you may find your previously attractive home in disrepair. At this juncture, your anger will be directed toward the puppy and you will again feel the anguish of defeat.

Many people have found that if you place a metal wind-up* clock or portable, battery-powered radio tuned to music or human voices in the bed with a very young puppy as you prepare it for the evening, the dog tends to rest more quietly. There are many theories

---

*Only a metal clock should be used, because even small puppies can gnaw on and totally destroy timepieces constructed of less durable materials. Similarly, only battery-powered radios should be used to prevent the possibility of accidental electrocution.

about this, but what matters is that the technique works in most cases and is worth trying.

What Your New Puppy Must Learn Now

Even very young puppies are capable of learning their names, elementary housebreaking (see page 62), and a few simple commands. This is also an excellent time to get your new pet accustomed to wearing a soft training collar and being led on a leash, and also to train it to be civilized in case it must be left unattended for a brief period. As was stated earlier, one should make every effort to see that a brand-new puppy is not left alone, but sometimes a brief absence is unavoidable.

Soon after you choose your puppy, you will probably settle on a name for it. The most suitable names for dogs contain no more than two syllables; ideally, the name should be monosyllabic. Each time you speak to the puppy, use its name in a normal conversational voice. Calling it by name will naturally lead to the command "Come!" Reinforce each successful lesson by giving verbal praise and softly stroking the puppy's head, neck, shoulders, and chest when it obeys your order. Negative or improper responses to your commands should summon your firm and immediate "No!" Most obedience trainers avoid corporal punishment, because it often only makes the new puppy fearful of you in particular, and humans in general.

As soon as you bring it home, the new puppy should wear a soft woven nylon training collar. The best collars are those fitted with a metal ring at each end. A soft, free-running loop is formed by placing one length of the collar into the ring at one end. The ring at the free end can

A well-behaved, properly trained Schnauzer does not beg for food during the family's mealtime.

then be attached to the snap-eye fastener at the end of the leash. Remember that, although your puppy will grow very rapidly, the collar will remain the same size; you must check it every few days and replace it as soon as it becomes even slightly snug on the dog's neck.

An alternative to the training collar is a head collar that encircles your puppy's muzzle and, when fitted properly, more directly controls movements of the head and neck without exerting pressure against the puppy's throat.

Leash training should be a gradual process, taking place over a day or two. Once the puppy has become accustomed to wearing its soft collar, attach the lightweight leash, and while you watch to see that it does not become entangled or snagged on projecting objects, allow the puppy to drag its leash around for a few minutes at a time. Again, reinforce the puppy's good behavior with verbal and gentle hand-stroking praise. Within a very brief time, the puppy will be used to the feel of the collar and the weight of the leash. Now you should take your new puppy outside to greet the world surrounding your home. At first, walk only a few yards. Remember that the tiny puppy has to take many more steps to equal one of your strides. If every brief outing is successful and pleasurable for both of you, each of you will soon look forward to leash-controlled walks. It is a delight to see a Schnauzer dance about in happy anticipation of an outing as soon as it sees you pick up its leash.

Even the very young puppy can and should be trained not to beg food from your dining table.

As part of your early training program, you must establish certain ground rules that your canine companion will not be allowed to break. Infringing on your meals by begging for snacks and handouts is a trait that is distasteful to many people. Moreover, the habit of allowing puppies to beg food from your table often leads to their refusal to accept commercially prepared dog food in favor of more tasty "people" food, to nutritional imbalances, and to canine obesity. The simplest way to discourage begging is merely to refuse even the most appealing whines and attempts to gain your attention. A firm "No!" and a forced return of the offending puppy to its sleeping basket or other site away from your immediate presence will usually convey your message of disapproval.

If a few table scraps are to be fed to your dog, they should be trimmed of all excess fat and should be mixed with the dog's regular food in such a fashion that they only partially flavor the commercial food, not take the place of it.

This handsome Giant has been carefully trained in good manners since early puppyhood; it is obvious that he is a real member of the family.

This Miniature was fortunate in that it was trained using positive reinforcement.

This Giant Schnauzer puppy will go through life with natural, uncropped ears. There is increasing support for natural ears among all the Schnauzer breeds.

The amount of attention you give your Schnauzer will reflect in its appearance and condition. This handsome black Miniature is an example of good care—inside and out.

A puppy wants, most of all, to please you, its "pack leader." By showing it what you want and giving ample praise for good performance, you set a lifelong pattern of good behavior which you can always enjoy.

A well-trained dog always justifies the effort made in its training.

Miniatures, the most popular of the Schnauzers, usually get along well with other pets at home and in public.

Obtaining Body Temperature

Your Schnauzer's normal body temperature ranges from 100.5 to 102.5°F (38–39.1°C). A rectal or digital thermometer is used to determine your dog's rectal temperature. If the procedure is done gently, it will not be unpleasant to your pet.

✔ With a glass thermometer, be certain to shake it down so the mercury column is below the 96°F (35.5°C) mark on the barrel.

✔ Lubricate the tip of the thermometer with a dab of petroleum jelly.

✔ Support your dog's rear quarters with one hand beneath and between its rear legs to prevent it from sitting.

✔ Gently insert the thermometer at least 2 inches (5.08 cm) into the dog's rectum.

A lubricated stubby rectal thermometer is gently inserted into your Schnauzer's rectum as you restrain your dog's tail.

✔ Leave a glass thermometer in place for two to three minutes.

✔ An electronic digital thermometer accurately records temperature within a few seconds after being inserted.

✔ After obtaining the temperature, clean the thermometer with an alcohol-moistened tissue.

✔ Shake the mercury down into the bulb of a glass thermometer, and replace it into its storage case.

Bathing

Folklore has spawned many grooming myths. Puppies need *not* reach a minimum age before their first bath. Young puppies should be bathed whenever they become soiled. A warm bath using mild soap readily cleanses the coat and skin.

✔ Place a drop or two of mineral oil into each eye to protect eyes from any chance of irritation if soap should enter them.

✔ Thoroughly lather the coat, removing any food residue or fecal matter.

✔ Completely rinse the soap from the coat. Make sure that no soap remains beneath the front or rear limbs or in your Schnauzer's ears.

✔ Dry the coat with an absorbent bath towel.

✔ If necessary, a hand-held hair dryer, *on a moderate setting* can be used to complete the drying. Do not direct the dryer's air stream into your Schnauzer's eyes, and do not leave a puppy unattended; it might chew the power cord and become electrocuted.

Grooming

✔ Between baths, regularly brush your Schnauzer's coat.

✔ Gently comb the eyebrows, mustaches, and chin whiskers to free them from tangles.

✔ If you start your dog's grooming at an early age and do it gently, it will enjoy these attentions. If you wait until your dog is already filthy and its coat is a mass of tangled knots, the grooming experience will be unhappy for both of you, and it should probably be done by a professional pet groomer.

Care of the Claws and Paws

A puppy's sharp claws normally wear themselves down on hard, abrasive surfaces, otherwise the claws will grow too long and may curl inward, thus injuring the soft toe pads.

✔ The first claw (dewclaw) corresponds to the human thumb and is set above the surface upon which the dog walks. Because of this, dewclaws tend to grow around and inward (like a ram's horn) unless they are periodically shortened.

✔ A dog's claws grow outward from a bed rich in blood vessels and nerves. If the claw is cut too short, it will bleed and cause pain.

✔ *Trim claws gradually, and remove only thin slices with a canine claw clipper.* Another benefit of going slowly is that it will build confidence in your Schnauzer.

Care of the Foot and Toe Pads

✔ Foot and toe pads may become abraded from running on rough surfaces, burned on hot pavement, punctured by thorns or slivers, or lacerated by broken glass or other sharp objects.

✔ If your dog limps or continually licks one or more of its feet, examine them carefully, and if possible, remove any foreign body you find.

Care of the Ears

✔ Earwax is normally secreted by the ear canals, and unless you are directed by your veterinarian to treat your Schnauzer's ear canals, do not interfere with them.

✔ Do not insert swabs into the ear canals.

✔ Ear mites and ear ticks occasionally parasitize canine ears and are readily treated.

✔ If medication is required, your veterinarian will give you instructions for applying it.

✔ Pet groomers may remove excessive ear-canal hair, if necessary. This procedure usually does not cause medical problems, but if not done carefully, it can induce temporary irritation.

Care of the Eyes

Other than cleaning mucus from the eyelids, you should not have to routinely care for your Schnauzer's eyes.

It is important to support your Schnauzer and keep it from sitting by placing your hand beneath its rear quarters until the thermometer is removed.

✔ Eyes affected by dust can be safely flushed with ophthalmic irrigation solution or sterile contact lens saline solution.

✔ *If eyelids are inflamed, or if your Schnauzer paws at its eyes excessively, there may be a foreign body present. Immediately consult your veterinarian for evaluation and treatment.*

Care of the Teeth

✔ Inspect your dog's teeth and gums weekly; your veterinarian will evaluate them during your Schnauzer's annual physical examination.

✔ A diet of hard biscuits or kibbled dog food inhibits accumulation of tartar and calculus.

✔ Soft foods tend to encourage tartar accumulation and gum irritation.

✔ Cracked, fractured, or abscessed teeth should be extracted.

✔ Professional teeth cleaning can be performed periodically.

✔ Regular toothbrushing with canine toothpaste at home may be necessary.

DAILY LIFE WITH YOUR SCHNAUZER

A puppy should be picked up by placing one hand around and beneath its chest, right in front of its forelimbs, and supporting the rear quarters with the other hand.

Lifting and Carrying the Dog

Be gentle when picking the puppy up; remember how you feel when an elevator rises too rapidly for your comfort. Although the puppy's dam may have picked it up by the scruff of the neck, the puppy is now older and heavier; if you employ this method, you probably will cause discomfort, if not outright pain. An older dog is best picked up, depending upon the size of the animal, by placing one hand or arm in front of the forelimbs and the other behind the rear limbs and lifting straight up in one steady movement. Sometimes it is useful to hold the two front legs together between the thumb and middle fingers of one

Many Schnauzers, particularly Miniatures, are acquired to be children's pets. And they are very good at it. However, children should be taught to approach their pets with kindness for the relationship to be successful.

hand; this maneuver helps steady the limbs and keeps the dog from struggling.

Injured dogs must be picked up very carefully so that 1) you will not cause additional pain, and 2) you can avoid causing the dog to injure you in an attempt to protect itself. In many, if not all, cases it is prudent to apply a soft gauze or cloth-strip binding around the injured dog's muzzle, cinching it just in front of the eyes. Several wraps of cloth are placed over and around the muzzle, tying the last two on top of and beneath the jaws. The last tie should be a bow knot so that it may be easily released when appropriate.

If a back injury is suspected, the dog should be gently placed upon a solid, unyielding object, such as a wide board or small door, that can serve as a litter.

Dogs and Children

The Schnauzer has been recognized for many years as a suitable breed to be in a household with children because of its native intelligence,

This is the proper way to carry a Schnauzer puppy. The hindquarters are supported with one hand while the forefeet are restrained with the fingers and thumb of the other hand.

further torment by aggressive behavior. This is an unusual state for a normally tolerant Schnauzer.

The breed naturally makes a splendid watchdog; this trait could at times create a situation where a child might by his or her actions cause a dog to act in a manner that could result in injury to the youngster. Disturbing any dog while it is eating is unwise, and children should be cautioned about this. A child may be allowed to remove the dog's food and water bowls after the dog has finished using them. There is no reason why a child cannot be trained how to brush a dog gently and do other simple tasks that will help instill confidence in both the child and dog.

Be careful of balls or other playthings carelessly tossed over your backyard fence: If they are retrieved by a stranger, it could trigger a defensive reaction, which is normal for your Schnauzer's natural watchdog tendencies. When a stranger arrives at the door of your home, the dog should be restrained so that it will not act impulsively toward an unfamiliar person. When your Schnauzer is on a leash outside of your home or is in your automobile, it may be approached by strangers who wish to pet it. This is only natural, but it is important that the dog be allowed to sniff the back of the hand of the person and be given the opportunity to react before actual hand contact is made with it. This also affords the person time to withdraw the proffered hand in case the dog does not wish to be touched. This

responsiveness to the wishes of its human companions, and loyalty. This is not to promise that all Schnauzers will immediately show fondness for every child they encounter. Our own first Miniature Schnauzer displayed what can only be termed genuine affection for our own children, but barked and exhibited wariness at the approach of all other small children who were not part of our family. This is only natural. Over the years we have always brought our dogs aboard our houseboat as we plied the waters of the Sacramento-San Joaquin River delta system, and each has proven herself a very seaworthy member of our crew. Our Schnauzer and Yorkshire Terriers were particularly sensitive to the high-pitched piping voices of small children, even though these dogs were brought up with small children. It seems that the voices of some small children may be an irritant to some dogs. Some children will tease a dog to the point where the animal's patience is exhausted and it seeks to protect itself from is particularly important in the case of exuberant young children who are unaware of how to approach a strange dog.

Very young children should never be left unattended with a dog. This precaution protects both child and dog from accidents. Once an older child has demonstrated that he or she knows how to treat your dog with respect and the dog has reacted positively to that child, they may be left to play together from time to time, but adult supervision should be close by in case it is required.

Dogs and a New Baby

If you are anticipating imminent parenthood and already have a resident Schnauzer, you are about to be twice blessed!

Under most circumstances, your dog should be introduced to the baby as soon as possible after bringing your new heir home. Remember, the dog had been a surrogate "only child" before the birth of the baby, and it is only natural for the dog to express some jealousy if, after arriving home with a new baby, you totally ignore the presence of your canine companion. It is a good idea to allow your dog to see and to sniff the baby's scent, but not lick the baby. Make certain while making this introduction that you praise the dog and tell it how good it is behaving. If you follow these simple steps, dogs will almost invariably bond with the newest addition to their "pack" and begin to demonstrate not only great interest

Your Schnauzer's first introduction to other household pets is important. Remain with and reassure them both by petting and speaking to them in a calm voice.

and devotion, but also an immediate tendency to guard the baby from any perceived threat from outside your household. It is most gratifying to witness these wonderful traits of the Schnauzer, and you will be happy that you have taken the time to make the introduction.

Since some parasites can be transmitted from dogs to humans, it is wise, before the anticipated arrival of your new baby, to have your dog's stools microscopically examined for parasitic worm ova and protozoa.

Many of us have grown up with a least one dog in our family, and we appear to have been well served psychologically from our early experiences!

Dogs and Other Pets

It is natural for a dog to show intense interest in other animals. Some dogs will bond strongly to other dogs, cats, even guinea pigs, hamsters, rats, mice, rabbits, and birds. Remember, though, that some of these other animals were the natural prey of the dog's ancient ancestors. There can be no guarantee that a given Schnauzer will accept another animal (or, for that matter, another human) as a friend. The primary concept is that the initial introduction can be all-important to the future relationship. Just as with a new baby in the family, it is vital to make the introduction of

a new pet a positive one for the resident dog. Show it how much you care for it by saying the dog's name and petting it while handling the new animal. Allow it to see and smell the newcomer and, if appropriate, even lick it.

Dogs can be easily introduced to kittens, and adult cats often adopt new puppies without too much fuss. It is only when both the dog and the cat are adults when first introduced to each other that problems arise.

You may find that the dog prefers to eat the cat's food. If this behavior is observed, you need only place the cat's food dish on a high place where the cat can reach it, but the dog cannot. Commercial cat food often contains a higher protein level than is necessary for dogs; its consumption by your Schnauzer should be discouraged. Besides, your dog just might develop a preference for it, refusing to eat dog food.

A Second Dog?

In my opinion, there are no compelling reasons for not having two dogs in the same household; if there were, I would be guilty of hypocrisy because we have had as many as three dogs at one time. The *timing* of the acquisition of a second dog is of great importance. Just as children do, puppies readily learn good and bad habits from their older siblings or peers. For this reason, it is usually better to bring a puppy into a home in which there is already a relatively mature dog. The early training of the new animal will be easier as it observes the behavior of its older canine tutor. This is particularly true with respect to housebreaking and obedience training. It is a delight to witness this process in action. For example, the first of our dogs to learn to swim to our boat, then climb straight up a vertical four-step ladder, was one of our Yorkshire Terriers, Shibui (Japanese for *understated elegance*). Within a day or two she had taught, by example, one of our Miniature Schnauzers to mimic her behavior. Soon their example had been copied by another of our dogs, a noble mongrel of dubious ancestry. Before long, people would wade to our boat, timidly knock on the hull, and ask to see the dogs who were becoming famous because they routinely "jumped ship," swam ashore to relieve themselves, then swam back to the houseboat, climbed the ladder, and hopped back aboard. Soon these dogs were the subjects of videotapes depicting "smart" dog tricks! Alas, we cannot take credit for this show of obvious canine cleverness, because one of our dogs had discovered that a boat's boarding ladder was no impediment to returning "home."

It is vital when first introducing the new puppy to an older resident dog to avoid instilling a feeling of jealousy or partiality. As when

The safest way to transport a dog is in a secure crate. If your vehicle can fit a crate comfortably, you should invest in one for your Schnauzer.

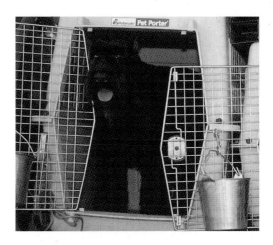

introducing a new baby to a resident dog, make certain to praise the older dog so it knows it is being noticed at the same time that so much attention is being given to the newcomer.

When feeding the puppy, take time to give the older dog a snack of dry kibble. Unless the older dog has kidney or heart disease, puppy food will do no harm. The few extra calories will, for a week or so, be expended in the extra exercise playing with the puppy. Follow the directions on the container of the puppy food with respect to the amount and frequency of feeding. The two dogs should be fed from separate dishes, but they may share the same water bowl and sleeping quarters. In fact, by allowing the two dogs to sleep together, you will avoid the problem of the youngster not wanting to sleep in its bed, but instead wanting to follow you into your bedroom.

Like children, puppies are stimulated to urinate and defecate shortly after they eat. Also, because they are immature, their ability to retain a full urinary bladder and colon is limited in comparison to a grown dog. For this reason it is important to take the youngster out for a leash-controlled walk soon after it has eaten. The older dog should also be taken

out, even if it does not have to eliminate. With one leashed dog on either side of you, a routine of businesslike behavior will soon be established, so that these communal walks will result in almost immediate productivity, rather than sight-seeing excursions. The young puppy should be taken out in the evening for its last exercise and be given the opportunity to relieve itself just before being put to bed. This will help train it to retain its wastes throughout the night.

Most Schnauzers enjoy car trips whether they mean around the block or across the country. When including your Schnauzer in your travel plans, be sure the dog is safely restrained so he is not a danger to himself or to any human passengers.

It is only natural for mild conflicts to arise between any two animals; occasionally, a younger animal, as it grows to adulthood, will gain dominance. At first, this elevated rank many manifest itself in the selection of favored toys, food, sleeping arrangements, and aggressive play. When playing with the dogs together, try to fairly give each dog its equal share of your attention.

Travel by Automobile, Train, and Air

Coping with and Preventing Motion Sickness

Having vacationed for years with our own dogs aboard our houseboat, I can heartily champion the inclusion of the family dog(s) in those vacation plans in which a canine companion would represent a bonus rather than a burden. One must always be aware of a few factors.

Once they are accustomed to vehicular travel, most dogs eagerly anticipate each opportunity to go for rides—unless these trips are only to the veterinarian's office! Inexperienced canine travelers, like their human counterparts, must gradually develop a tolerance of motion. The easiest way to condition a dog to motion is to take it on very brief trips of only a few blocks, gradually lengthening trips to several miles as the dog develops a tolerance. When starting this training, schedule the outing before feeding time.

Be vocal in your encouragement; praise your Schnauzer for being a fine companion. Attach the dog's leash to its collar so that there will be a natural association with a forthcoming outing.

Motion sickness does not suddenly manifest itself by immediate explosive vomiting; it has warning signs. One of the first signs of threatening nausea is salivation and frequent swallowing movements. At the first evidence of this behavior, immediately park your car and allow the dog to get out and walk around with its leash on. Usually only a few minutes are required to reestablish the middle ear's equilibrium and settle your canine companion's queasiness. As soon as your Schnauzer seems to be normal again, place it back into your car and drive until signs of early nausea return. Repeat this process over and over and, within a few days, even a very young dog will become a seasoned traveler, ever ready to accompany you on your excursions. Once your dog is accustomed to automobile trips, it is but a minor step to travel by train and airplane.

Even the experienced canine traveler seems to fare better if it is fed at the end of the trip, rather than just before departure.

If you must take a trip with your Schnauzer before it has been conditioned to travel, it may be given medication to reduce its sensitivity to motion. Some common antinausea drugs are available from your veterinarian, who will provide you with instructions and information on how to make your Schnauzer's trip as pleasant as possible. They are relatively safe, but in high dosages will induce sleepiness and the inability of a dog to regulate its body temperature. Generally $\frac{1}{8}$ to $\frac{1}{4}$ of a small child's dosage is sufficient to inhibit motion sickness in a Miniature Schnauzer. Adult Giant or Standard Schnauzers will require as much as $\frac{1}{2}$ to a full tablet. Your family veterinarian can also prescribe or dispense mild tranquilizer tablets that will help prevent motion sickness.

Ideally, anti–motion sickness medications should be given at least one hour before the anticipated departure time. As an alternative to medication for preventing motion sickness, you can give your Schnauzer one or more small capsules of dried ground ginger root. This common herb is available at health food stores and has shown promise as an anti–motion sickness agent. It has the advantage of not inducing drowsiness. The dosage is not critical because any excess will be metabolized as a nutrient.

When travel aboard a train or commercial airplane is anticipated, be certain to inquire from the carrier what arrangements and airline rules must be followed. Your dog will probably be confined to an approved shipping crate. As is the case with automobile travel, food should be withheld before departure. Water can be offered until approximately one hour before the dog must be crated. A leashed walk will encourage your Schnauzer to empty its bladder and move its bowels.

Items to Be Included in the Luggage

Depending upon whether your travel is by automobile, train, airplane, or ship, you may have to pack a supply of your Schnauzer's regular dog food, an appropriate food dish, and a water bowl. If you travel by automobile, a plastic bottle of water will free you from having to locate a source of uncontaminated water. A warm blanket or washable heavy cotton bath towel, your dog's leash, and grooming utensils also should be packed.

If veterinary prescription medications are being given to your Schnauzer, it is imperative that you pack a supply to last the entire length of the trip; it might be difficult to refill prescriptions away from home. A container of a nonprescription antidiarrhea medication is

a welcome addition to the kit. Constipation is an unusual problem, but if your traveling dog experiences difficulty in defecation, a small amount of milk of magnesia usually brings relief. A container of anti–flea and tick spray or powder should be considered if your itinerary will take you where an infestation is likely.

In case of accident, first aid supplies suitable for human use are appropriate for emergency veterinary care.

Travel Abroad

Securing the Appropriate Travel Documents

If you plan to travel abroad with your dog, inquire of the airlines, shipping company, or railroad about special documentation required for international transit. You will also have to check with the consulate or embassy of each nation whose territory you will travel through. Permits for animal transit will depend upon standard health examination and certification that your dog is not harboring infectious disease. These permits generally expire after 31 days and may have to be renewed by one or more foreign veterinary inspectors. A complete set of your dog's health records that document vaccinations is essential. In most instances, booster injections should be administered two to three weeks before your anticipated departure.

Some countries impose a prolonged entry quarantine period for as long as six months. This is at your expense and you cannot remove your dog from the quarantine facility until the full prescribed period has expired. You should also know that you will not have any right of appeal of these regulations.

WHEN YOUR FEMALE IS IN HEAT

Most sexually mature female dogs experience two periods of potential reproductive activity per year. Some females may go through only one annual cycle; others may have as many as three.

The Estrus Cycle

The stages of the normal canine estrus cycle are called, in sequence, *proestrus, estrus, diestrus* (or, if conception has occurred, *pregnancy*) and, finally, *anestrus*. Each of these phases will be described briefly.

Proestrus is a preparatory phase of the cycle characterized by increased activity of the ovaries and uterus. Within the ovaries eggs are maturing, the lining of the uterus becomes more vascular and thickened, and finally a blood-tinged discharge is seen issuing from the vagina. The external genitalia of the female, called the vulva, become swollen to perhaps twice normal, quiescent size. This phase lasts four to thirteen days; average length is nine days. Although

If you got your Schnauzer as a pet, resist the temptation to breed. You will do yourself and your dog a favor to have it neutered following your veterinarian's recommendations.

superficially similar in some of its outward manifestations, proestrus in the female is not equivalent to menstruation in humans. Although the discharge attracts male dogs to the female at this time, she usually will not allow them to mount and breed her.

Estrus follows proestrus in a subtle manner. The vulva remains enlarged and the vaginal discharge becomes less blood-tinged, until it is entirely clear and resembles thin mucus. In some cases there may be a yellowish discharge, but this is not a reason to be concerned unless it becomes copious or continues for more than two weeks. Male dogs are even more avidly drawn to the female at this time, and most often she will allow males to mount and mate with her. As the eggs mature, the ovaries increase their secretion of estrogenic hormones. Ovulation, the actual release of ripe eggs from the ovaries into the oviducts and eventually into the uterus, occurs some time between the ninth and the fourteenth day, counting from the very first day of observed proestrus. Like the length of proestrus, estrus continues for about nine to thirteen days, and although the female may remain receptive to courting males throughout the full time of estrus, the mature released eggs are capable of being fertilized by sperm for only a limited time of about four to six days.

If fertilization occurs, the ovarian secretion of progesterone continues and the uterus remains receptive to the implantation and development of fertilized eggs. It takes from six to ten days for the fertilized eggs to reach the uterine "horns" after ovulation. Here they become partially imbedded within the rich vascular lining of the uterine walls. The newly fertilized eggs soon become embryos and, later, fetuses.

If conception does not occur, the uterus enters another stage where it gradually becomes less vascular and relatively inactive. The ovarian hormone secretion changes from mostly progesterone to mostly estrogen.

Diestrus lasts about two months. During this phase, the mammary glands are prepared to secrete milk. Sometimes nonpregnant females will exhibit swelling of their breast tissues and nipples. Both pregnant and nonpregnant females may construct nests at this time and they may show their strong maternal instincts by carrying inanimate objects such as socks into these nests and appearing to nuzzle and try to nurse them, as if they were puppies. A slight sticky discharge may be noticed seeping from the nipples at this time. Diestrus usually lasts from 80 to 90 days following the initiation of proestrus.

Anestrus is the last phase of the estrous cycle. It begins at the close of diestrus and is a period of inactivity. The uterus shrinks markedly during this time and the ovaries are quiescent. Anestrus persists for approximately two to four months in most females, but this interval is quite variable. If pregnancy and nursing have continued to completion, anestrus will be delayed for their duration.

As mentioned earlier, chlorophyll tablets are available that, when given to females very early in their proestrus, will greatly diminish the sexually attractive odor of their vaginal discharges.

Although hormone injections and tablets that will postpone the onset of proestrus and estrus in females are available from some veterinarians, I do not recommend their use because they carry with them a significant risk of hormonal imbalance, uterine infections, and eventual sterility.

If you do not wish to breed your Schnauzer female at this time, you have several alternatives to having every sexually mature male dog in the neighborhood camp on your doorstep. Often the chlorophyll tablets will be all that is necessary to render your female less desirable to these erstwhile suitors. A pair of protective panties that contain a pocket for holding a changeable absorptive pad may be purchased or

Each year millions of unwanted dogs are put to sleep in the United States.

constructed at home. If you have to physically separate your female from your home until she is no longer so attractive to males, she may be placed in a boarding kennel for a week or so.

In the sad event that all of your efforts at keeping your female chaste are abject failures and she is accidentally bred to a dog that, for any number of reasons, is unsuitable, your veterinarian can administer injections that will prevent implantation of the fertilized eggs. Often these injections will greatly accentuate the signs of estrus, but even if she is bred again within a few days, she is very unlikely to conceive.

These injections can—and often do—produce unintended consequences in the form of pseudopregnancy (pseudocyesis), uterine inflammation and infection (pyometritis, pyometra), and mammary gland tenderness and swelling, sometimes inducing milk production and mastitis. It is for these reasons that many veterinarians, the author included, prefer not to administer these drugs.

Because of the great effort and time that it takes to properly care for a female and her puppies, amateur breeding is discouraged. The major upset to a household that occurs with the end of gestation and eventual delivery and care for a litter of demanding puppies can be substantial. Furthermore, for the Schnauzer breed to be continually improved genetically requires the services of those skilled in the selection of suitable breeding stock with outstanding physical and psychological traits.

One last comment: There is no shortage of puppies needing good homes in the United States today. Literally thousands of unwanted puppies and adult dogs are destroyed *every day* because of a gross imbalance between oversupply and inadequate demand. No one should worsen this situation by producing yet more puppies, no matter how appealing the idea seems at first.

False Pregnancy: Explanation and Solutions

False pregnancy can affect any mature female animal. In affected dogs, serious psychological abnormalities accompany the physiologic disturbances. The causes for this disorder include ovarian cysts and associated ovarian hormone dysfunction and pituitary hormone imbalances. The condition resembles many of the outward signs of normal pregnancy. There may even be uterine or other abdominal contractions mimicking true labor. A nest is made and objects are carried into the nest, serving as surrogate puppies. These are protected by the female from "intruders."

Some cases of pseudopregnancy (pseudocyesis) yield to conservative internal therapy, but others require far more aggressive treatment. Some affected dogs may develop a condition called *pyometritis* and/or *pyometra,* where the uterus becomes severely inflamed, and may, if the cervix remains closed, fill with pus. Often, intense thirst and increased urination are symptomatic. This is most serious and may require surgical removal of the ovaries and uterus; it is far more involved than routine sterilization.

The only sure prevention is spaying female puppies before first estrus. Pyometritis and pyometra most often affect females that have never had a litter—a common factor in pseudo-pregnancy, Although occurrence can be spontaneous, it can be induced by administration of hormone-containing antimating or abortion drugs.

THE PROPER DIET

Several conscientious animal feed companies have expended a great amount of time, energy, and money on formulating, testing, and marketing a variety of carefully balanced canine diets that, when fed exclusively, will completely meet or exceed the nutritional requirements for dogs.

Schnauzers Require Nutritious Dog Food

Commercial Foods

Some foods are more palatable than others, and you may find that for the same amount of money you can buy a substantially greater volume of one or two compared to others of equal nutritive value. Commercially prepared dog foods are supplied in dry, semimoist, and moist (canned) forms. The greatest difference between these three major divisions is their moisture content. High-quality canned foods are the most expensive when you compute their high moisture content, which often amounts to approximately 75 percent. This makes canned dog food a costly convenience. Individual packages of burger-like semimoist dog foods are lightweight, nutritious, and readily accepted by most dogs, but they contain some ingredients

Select a dog food for your Schnauzer that is complete and nutritionally balanced; don't leave the choice up to your pet.

that are of questionable value; in order to make certain that these products resist spoilage, they are formulated with sugar and sugarlike substances and propylene glycols. While neither of these classes of ingredients is now known to be harmful, there are some nutritional experts who doubt their safety in a regular diet. Furthermore, the canned and semimoist diets are too soft to give your dog's gums and teeth needed exercise. The remaining class of commercial diets is the dry kibble and meal type. Many are nearly as palatable as the canned and semimoist foods but have the added advantages of light weight per volume of product and firmness that provides jaw, gum, and tooth exercise. The larger sizes of kibble require active chewing that greatly aids in keeping the teeth clean and free of plaque and tartar accumulation.

Whatever commercial products you select, they will almost certainly be of greater nutritional value than scraps of food from your dining table. As mentioned earlier, occasional treats of fat-free, boned meat, fish, or fowl are welcome, but should not be fed as a staple to your Schnauzer because scraps may be grossly unbalanced with respect to vitamin, mineral, protein, fat, carbohydrate, and fiber content. Furthermore, dietary and gastrointestinal disturbances are much less likely to occur when dogs are fed scientifically formulated commercial diets.

The amount of food to be fed is determined by several factors: the stage of life; physical size of the dog; its metabolic size (which is not identical to weight); weather and/or housing arrangements in which the dog is maintained; reproductive activity; amount of exercise or work that the dog is expected to perform; and the comparative quality of the food itself.

Rapidly growing puppies eat much more food per unit of their body weight because they are synthesizing new tissues and expending an enormous amount of energy. The gross size of a dog will naturally dictate that larger dogs should be fed a greater volume of food than smaller ones, but the metabolic rates of smaller dogs are correspondingly higher than those of the so-called "giant" breeds. Dogs living outdoors in cold weather expend substantial energy just keeping warm. Both reproductively active stud male dogs and brood females must be fed a greater amount of high-quality food than animals of the same size and age who are not being employed as breeders. A lactating female will increase her dietary needs enormously because of the amount of energy expended in producing milk for her puppies. Hard-working dogs or those given much exercise require more total nutrients than more sedentary canines.

It is false economy to purchase the cheapest brand of dog food. Also, several serious physical disorders have been traced to some "generic" dog food brands. Some of these "nonbrand" animal feeds lack one or more essential nutri-

ents. Over the intermediate to long term, such so-called "bargain" brands will probably result in veterinary fees that far outweigh the modest savings that were realized originally.

Table Scraps

As mentioned earlier, scraps from your dining table may be prized by your dog as snacks, but should not be fed as a regular ration. Carefully boned and fat-trimmed lean meat scraps can be mixed with your dog's regular commercial dog food as a special treat. There is no question that most table scraps may be very palatable to your dog, but if they are fed too often, your canine companion may refuse to accept its own diet in the expectation that you will give in and feed it what you eat. Also, leftover "goodies" from parties are frequently found to be responsible for severe bouts of vomiting and/or diarrhea in pets.

Finally, there may be times when you wish to add some safe seasoning to your dog's otherwise bland fare. Special prescription diets formulated for older dogs or for those suffering from heart of kidney disease, intestinal disorders, or other problems do lack flavor. A small amount of garlic powder or dried onion flakes can substantially improve the special diet's palatability without changing its sodium salt or protein content.

Feeding a Puppy

Even before they are weaned, puppies will begin to nibble on kibbled puppy foods. By the time they are about six weeks old most of their dietary intake should consist of commercially prepared puppy fare. There are several major brands available in North America; despite

Fish, fowl, and other bones that splinter easily, and many table scraps can cause serious gastrointestinal upset when fed to dogs. Generally, scraps not suitable for human consumption should not be fed to your Schnauzer.

claims to the contrary by their manufacturers, there is little substantive difference among most of them. To date, however, new products have been developed to be fed throughout the entire lifetime of a dog, varying only the amount fed during any particular growth or maintenance life phase. All dog food manufacturers publish feeding instructions on the bags or boxes in which their products are shipped. These recommendations should be followed faithfully.

Some young puppies, and older dogs as well, do not tolerate cow's milk in its fresh whole or low-butterfat forms. This is because many animals lack a specific enzyme required to digest and assimilate milk sugar. Most of these milk-sensitive dogs will, however, tolerate cow's milk products such as buttermilk, yogurt, and cottage or farmer's cheese. Most dogs accept fresh goat's milk without the digestive upsets that are so characteristic of cow's milk consumption.

Feeding a Mature Dog

Once a dog has grown to maturity on a particular commercial diet, maintain this diet unless your veterinarian advises you to change to something else. The amount fed may have to be adjusted as changes in your Schnauzer's situation occur. Pregnancy, lactation, and strenuous work or exercise will necessitate increased food intake. Obesity and inactivity are indications for reducing the amount fed.

Some organ meats, especially liver, will induce diarrhea in many dogs. A small amount may be welcomed as a treat, but it must be cooked before feeding. Cooked beef heart is another good supplement to an otherwise standardized diet. It should be thoroughly boiled in a small volume of water, with a few sliced onions and carrots; the resulting broth can then be mixed with your dog's kibbled ration.

Over the years, we have always fed our dogs moderate amounts of fresh, raw vegetables and fruit—carrots, cabbage, rutabagas, broccoli, cauliflower, oranges, apples, and other produce in season. Freshly prepared unsalted popcorn and occasional almonds and peanuts are also special treats. These nutritious foods are rich in vitamins, minerals, and fiber and, with the exception of the nuts, are very low in calories. A confession: The major reason for feeding such items is that our dogs have always been very fond of them!

The folkloric notion that dogs need bacon grease or tallow to develop and maintain a sleek coat is foolishness; these saturated fats are no better for your dog than they are for you. All dogs require essential fatty acids, but these are readily available from far safer sources than high-cholesterol waste animal fats.

These puppies have inherited their physical appearance and the basis of their temperament from their parents. Their behavior will be further shaped by their environment as they grow.

Enjoy your Schnauzer for itself. If you decide on a companion for it, you can purchase another Schnauzer, acquire one from Schnauzer rescue or adopt from your local shelter.

When your dog is properly fed, its condition will speak for the quality of its diet.

These Standard Schnauzers keep a watchful eye on their home turf.

With a nutritious diet, adequate exercise and regular grooming your Schnauzer will maintain its great vitality, enabling it to join you in numerous activities.

Schnauzers love being out of doors. Make sure your pet gets every bit of time you can give for its recreation.

General Feeding Tips

Young growing dogs should be fed 5 to 6 times a day until they are about 8 to 10 weeks old and 3 to 4 times a day until they are 12 to 14 weeks old; twice daily until they are about 6 months old; and once daily thereafter.

In our household, we have always fed our adult dogs in the morning. By evening time, they have digested and assimilated their meal and, after their last evening walk or run, have passed their stools.

Only enough food should be placed in the dish that can be consumed during a 15-minute period. This will encourage your Schnauzer to be businesslike and goal-oriented in its eating habits, without inducing it to bolt its food.

If nondisposable food dishes are used, they must be cleaned routinely to remove any traces of uneaten food. The water bowl should be cleaned and refilled at least once daily, more often if it becomes contaminated with food particles washed from your Schnauzer's mustaches and chin whiskers.

In actual practice there is no right or wrong time to schedule the feeding of an adult dog. The most important consideration is that feeding should take place at about the same time and in the same place every day. Of course, there will always be those times when you are called away unexpectedly, must work late or must deal with a specific emergency. Your Schnauzer will not be adversely affected by occasional variation; just make it a point not to feed any old time or when the spirit moves you. In feeding, as in all else, dogs are very much creatures of habit and should not be made subject to anxiety because of a fluctuating or non-existent feeding schedule.

The wise dog owner will approach feeding with a definite system. A dependable, consistent schedule is an excellent start, but there is more to consider. Dogs are endowed with a wonderful sense of what is happening around them and will respond appropriately. Schnauzers can be extra sensitive by normal dog standards. Your consistent movements will signal to your bewhiskered friend that you are getting ready to prepare food. So when you have your movements down, keep to your routine. Feed in the same place, using the same utensils and give your Schnauzer the same food pan for all its meals. You and your Schnauzer will both be happier for it.

The number of meals your adult dog is fed in any 24-hour period is very much subject to the convenience of you, its owner. Conventional wisdom tells us to feed an adult dog one substantial meal every day, but your individual circumstances may dictate that your Schnauzer should be fed two, or even three times a day. If someone is in the home all day, multiple feedings become more feasible, but if you feed just one meal, it may help to give your dogs a couple of biscuits or a raw carrot to break the long interval between meals.

If your Schnauzer is a Giant or even a Standard, you might want to use the two-meal regimen as a protection against the possibility of bloat. More formally known as Gastric Dilation-Volvulus (GDV), bloat is a very painful and dangerous condition in which the stomach twists over on itself, trapping food, liquid, and gas. Once the stomach is twisted tightly enough to cut off the blood supply, death can result in a very short time. Happily, there are several effective ways to safeguard your dog. The condition seems to affect larger, deep-chested dogs and is believed to be related to heredity and individual temperament.

The Five Essential Nutrient Groups

Nutrient/Found in...	Dietary Function/ Deficiency Symptoms
Protein Animal sources—red meat, fowl, dairy products, fish Vegetable sources—wheat germ, soybean products, brewer's yeast	Furnish amino acids required for growth, overall development, healthy bones and musculature; enhance production of enzymes antibodies as well as hormones; **deficiencies**—subnormal growth, weight loss, anorexia, poor coat condition.
Fat Animal sources—vegetable oils	Furnish energy: furnish essential fatty acids and the fat-soluble vitamins A, D, E, and K; enhance taste of food essential for healthy skin and coat; **deficiencies**—dry, brittle coat, skin lesions.
Carbohydrates starches, sugars	Assist in regulation of energy balance; source of fiber for regulation of digestive system and normal bowel function.
Vitamins fruits, vegetables, fish liver oils, wheat germ oil, brewer's yeast	Furnish essential agents in preventing a wide variety of illnesses and disorders; important in regulation of many body functions such as growth and fertility.
Minerals/Trace Minerals meat, bones, grains, fruits, vegetables	Furnish essential agents in preventing a wide variety of illnesses and disorders; important in regulation of many body functions such as bone development and plays a part in the regulation of water balance within the body. (Trace minerals get their name for the small quantities required by the body for good health.)

In addition to feeding several smaller meals, moisten the dry food with water or broth or mix a small amount of canned dog food into the dry. Allow the moistened food to stand long enough to expand before feeding. Do not allow your dog to bolt its food or exercise vigorously for an hour or so after eating.

A dog suffering from bloat will show obvious signs of distress and must be seen by a veterinarian immediately. Talk to your veterinarian and your dog's breeder about bloat and what they recommend to prevent it.

Also with a Giant or Standard Schnauzer, you might want to invest in an elevated feeding platform that will allow your dog to eat more comfortably and with better posture.

Some dogs are comfortable eating in their crates. If you own more than one dog, consider this format to eliminate arguments at mealtimes and to allow your dogs to eat in a less stressful environment.

SIMPLE TRAINING

The type and amount of training you give your Schnauzer will vary based on your needs. You can be a benevolent dictator, but never give your dog the upper hand.

Adjusting to Collar and Leash

A soft training collar should be placed around your puppy's neck on the very first day that you bring it into your home. The popular varieties of pliant woven nylon collars, which are both lightweight and washable, are ideally suited for young Schnauzers. Frequently the puppy will not even notice that it is wearing it. Similarly, a leash is usually accepted—until it is used to direct the puppy in the direction in which *you* wish to walk! Typically, a naïve puppy will pull in every direction except the one in which you wish to go. With encouragement and positive reinforcement, even especially stubborn puppies will learn to be led while tethered to you by a leash.

The new head collar is another humane and effective training device.

It is imperative that you never use the leash as a punitive object. Your puppy should not associate a leash with unpleasantness.

All the Schnauzers are very bright and learn quickly. Be fair in your training, but never allow the dog to take the upper hand.

Correcting Bad Habits

Even the very best mannered dog will, on occasion, behave in a fashion that is contrary to your wishes. Remember that dogs are intelligent creatures and Schnauzers are especially bright and responsive to their human companions.

Once you perceive that your dog has developed a negative behavioral trait, it is important that you correct it in a manner that will convey to your pet that what it is doing will not be tolerated by you. You must be consistent in correction, and each time you apply corrective action it must be aimed at instruction rather than punishment. Even a young dog, if properly socialized, will strive to please its owner.

Jumping on People

Few things are more frightening to young children, or more annoying to adults, than to have a dog jump up on them. A dog's claws can cause deep scratches in tender skin, and a set of muddy pawprints rarely is welcomed by anyone wearing (previously) clean clothes.

A firm command, *"Down!"* delivered together with an immediate movement of one of your

A gentle, yet firm bump is delivered from your knee to your dog's chest as a correction for jumping on people.

knees so that it strikes the offending dog squarely on its upended chest, need only be done a few times to convey the correction.

Although this might seem to be a harsh correction, it has been recommended for generations by professional dog trainers, and it is not inhumane. Your knee only has to come into firm, but gentle, contact with your dog's chest to reinforce your verbal command. Once the dog has learned, you can provide positive reinforcement with praise and a small treat.

If your dog merely places its forepaws on you as it stands, say *"Down!"* as you gently place the pressure of your foot on the dog's rear toes. Your dog will soon learn that what it has been doing will not be tolerated by you or other humans.

Inappropriate Barking

It is entirely normal—and positive—for your dog to bark at strange sounds or people, but incessant howling or baying, particularly at night, is justifiable cause for complaints from your neighbors.

When this behavior occurs, you must immediately command, *"No!"* and comfort your dog so that it can see that there is no threat to you from outside. If necessary, command the dog to lie down near you, and each time it begins to vocalize, repeat the correction.

If your neighbors complain that your dog barks in your absence, you will have to take severe action to stop this disturbance once and for all. There are electronic devices built in to dog collars that, when activated by the sound of the dog's own bark, will deliver a mild shock to the skin immediately beneath the collar's electrodes. In some instances, these collars can be rented for a specified time from your veterinarian or local pet shop.

In the past, the "debarking" operation was often thought to be inhumane and, when not performed correctly, this procedure did not last. The state-of-the-art ventriculochordectomy, when performed by an experienced and skilled veterinary surgeon, is highly effective and, in this author's opinion, a humane and viable alternative to an electronic collar or disposal of the offensively barking dog. My family and I were avid houseboaters for more than a quarter century and we were always accompanied by our crew of small female Schnauzers, which, because of their terrier-like nature, tended to be excellent, though vocal, watchdogs. At the time I spayed them, I also debarked them, thus sparing them a second anesthetic and second operation. They continued to go through the motions of barking, without the attending din. All that could be heard through a closed door was a soft, cough-like sound. Inside our home, we could hear when our Schnauzers announced the arrival of visitors, but our neighbors heard nothing. These surgeries were performed when they were about 12 weeks old, and the effect was permanent without any complications.

Begging for Food

When you or other people are eating in your dog's presence, you and your guests should not be annoyed by begging. Your dog's nutritional needs are best met by its professionally formulated dog food, not from handouts from your dinner table.

A firm *"No!"* or *"Down!"* delivered with conviction is the appropriate correction for this behavior. Remember that you must be consistent. If begging was wrong yesterday, it will not be tolerated today or tomorrow, and you must not give in to those imploring brown eyes staring up from beneath your chair or table. It is equally important that other household members or guests not feed your Schnauzer.

Biting and Other Overaggressive Behavior

Although Standard and Miniature Schnauzers characteristically are not overly aggressive dogs, this guidebook would be incomplete without some discussion.

Even as very young puppies, some members of a litter will display dominance over their more submissive siblings, but once they have been weaned and placed into new homes, *they* should be submissive to their human companions, not vice versa. If your Schnauzer puppy exhibits a tendency to bite or in some other way acts in an aggressive manner to humans, you must correct it immediately and, with resolute firmness, give a loud, meaningful

command *"No!" "Out!"* or *"Aus!"* It is important to keep commands to a single syllable to avoid confusing your trainee.

In summary, your loud and firm verbal commands will often be all that is needed to correct aggressive misbehavior.

Inappropriate Chewing

It is entirely normal behavior for a puppy to explore its immediate environment by whatever means it has at its disposal. Dogs, being creatures possessing acute senses of smell and taste, will employ these to evaluate things novel to their limited experience. This exploration, no matter how normal, can be a source of danger to the animal and annoyance to you, its owner.

The most simple method for controlling chewing is to keep valuable items away from your puppy. Pick up belongings that might be chewed if left within the reach of the puppy. Try to redirect the puppy's inclination to chew

An alternative method for correcting a dog that jumps on people is to gently step on its hind toes while holding the front feet.

It is essential to train a dog to remain on its own property.

There are two solutions to this problem: For the short term, a loud and firm command of *"No!"* accompanied by banishment to the yard or another room often is satisfactory; for the longer term, surgical neutering might be appropriate. Unless you have some compelling reasons for breeding your male dog, there are many sound reasons why you should consider—and act on—the long-term solution. (This is discussed in greater detail in the section on spaying and neutering. See pages 73–74.)

by providing a few things that were meant to be gnawed. Rawhide chew bones or toys are excellent and will last for a variable time. If portions of them are chewed and are swallowed, they will be digested as food. Tough nylon chew bones are also available from pet suppliers and are nearly indestructible, but of course they are not digestible if swallowed.

Inappropriate Sexual Activity

The sexually motivated instincts of male dogs originate in a particularly ancient portion of the brain and are less readily modified by learned behavior corrections. It is only natural for a sexually mature dog to react to sexually arousing stimulation. Some dogs will mount and attempt to mate with stuffed toys, pillows, or a person's lower leg. This behavior may be triggered by any number of different stimuli. One frequent cause is the scent of a female in estrus. In some highly sensitive male dogs, this behavior can be induced when the dog perceives the scent of a menstruating woman.

Chasing Cars and Bicycles

Not only is the habit of chasing cars and bicycles a substantial danger to the dog, but it also is a hazard to the humans riding in the automobiles or on the bicycles. Responsible dog owners will do everything possible to prevent and stop their dogs from engaging in this behavior.

In some states a dog owner is held financially responsible for losses caused by the animal's uncontrolled behavior.

If you cannot or will not confine your dog to a fenced yard and it has developed the habit of chasing vehicles, you will have to use other restraints. One arrangement that allows freedom within a limited perimeter is a long leash attached to a large metal ring fastened to a horizontal wire like a clothesline.

Some dog trainers have advised having an accomplice armed with a toy squirt gun loaded with dilute lemon juice or a very mild aqueous ammonia solution purposely ride by on a bicycle several times until the dog runs out and starts to chase; at this point, the cyclist squirts the dog in the face. Although in legal terms this might be interpreted as entrapment, it is very effective; after one or two experiences of having a disagreeable yet harmless substance sprayed in the face, most dogs will soon associate the event of chasing with the distasteful correction.

More Severe Disciplinary Problems

Rarely is a dog owner faced with a disciplinary or behavioral problem that cannot be resolved by simple home obedience training. Some people, however, are just not capable of showing authority—even to a dog; others, for one reason or another, cannot discipline a dog. In these instances, it is best to seek the counsel of a professional dog trainer.

If a professional trainer finds deep-seated psychological abnormalities in your dog, you may wish to "cut your losses" before going further along an impossible path. Mental illness is known to affect animals, but the psychoanalytic methods of human therapy are not appropriate to dogs.

Teaching Some Practical Commands

Sit!

Place the puppy, while attached to its leash, on your left side. As you give the command "Sit!" place your hand firmly behind the knee area of its rear legs, pushing downward. Repeat this maneuver, each time commanding the dog to "Sit!" until your puppy will obey your command without having to be pushed down on its

A dog to walk at heel should also be trained to sit when the owner stops walking.

hocks. Each time the puppy successfully obeys and sits on command, give it lavish praise, petting it, and telling it what a splendid creature it is. A small treat will provide useful positive reinforcement of your verbal praise.

Stay!

One of the most useful commands that you can teach your Schnauzer is to *stay* in place—even when you walk away. Place your hand palm toward and close to the dog's face and command "Stay!" in a firm voice. Start to move away after a few moments, and if the puppy begins to follow you, stop immediately and repeat the command and hand signal. Again, giving a small, tasty treat reinforces your lavish praise for a job performed well.

Down!

Your dog should be trained to lie down immediately with its front legs extended in front of it. It can, if you desire, be a natural

progression from the *sit* command or can be used independently. Give the authoritative command *"Stay!"* as you place your hand on your dog's shoulders and apply gentle, yet firm, pressure downward. You then should stand in front of the dog and praise it for a job well done. Allow the dog to get up after a short while, and repeat the command and hand pressure until the dog obeys without hesitation. Give your canine pupil a small treat for obeying your command flawlessly.

Heel!

The well-mannered Schnauzer should walk, whether leashed or free, alongside your left leg. This is a standardized position and was developed to prevent your dog from tripping you by crossing your path. As you walk, use the leash to direct and keep the dog next to your left leg. While walking, turn to your left in a circle. Because the dog now finds itself inside of the circle, it will find that maintaining its position on your left is the easiest. When you stop walking forward, command the dog to *"Sit!"* Again, this is the conventional way a well-trained dog should behave.

Come!

This very important command is taught by starting with your dog in the *sit* or *down* position. After the dog is settled in one of these positions, command it to *"Stay!"* Take a few steps away, turn to face your dog, and drop to a kneeling or squatting position. Beckoning with your hands, say *"Come!"* in a soft, encouraging voice. Using a long leash to help guide your Schnauzer to come toward you often helps in early training. If the dog leaves its sitting or reclining position and obeys your

come command, praise it lavishly. Be absolutely certain, while teaching your dog this command, not to act in a negative fashion. It is imperative that you teach this particular command using only positive reinforcement, because if your dog becomes fearful of this request of yours, it may hesitate to come when it might be vital for it to do so. When your dog obeys your command and comes to you without hesitation, give it a small treat as a reward, in addition to your verbal praise.

Roll Over!

This simple command is very useful to teach your Schnauzer; at your instruction the dog will assume a position allowing you to inspect its belly for fleas, ticks, or foreign bodies attached to the skin or fur.

While your dog is already lying down, command it to *"Roll over!"* as you gently grasp its front legs and turn it onto its back and then over to the other side. Repeat the command several times; as you do it, roll your pet over onto its back. Praise each practice attempt, particularly when your dog rolls over without you using its legs as a prompt.

Fetch an Object

Most dogs will chase a moving object because it is their nature to pursue moving prey. Retrieving an object at your command is one of the easiest tricks to teach your dog.

Start with a rubber ball small enough to be easily carried in your dog's mouth, but large enough to prevent its being swallowed.

Command your dog to *"Sit!"* and praise it. Allow your pet to smell the ball. While your Schnauzer's attention is focused on the ball, throw it gently as you give the command *"Fetch!"*

If your dog immediately chases the ball and returns it to you, be lavish in your praise. If the dog ignores the ball entirely or merely dawdles, pick up the ball and repeat the exercise. You may allow the dog to taste the ball by placing it in its mouth.

Once you have taught your dog to run after and pick up the ball, command the dog to *"Come!"* back to you and to *"Sit!"* in front of you. As soon as it has assumed the sitting position, gently remove the ball from its jaws and praise it heartily. Repeat the entire sequence as many times as necessary. Dogs usually will learn this trick within a day or two.

After it has mastered *fetch* with the ball, you can substitute a rolled or folded newspaper. Soon you will able to command your Schnauzer to fetch your newspaper from where the delivery person deposited it. Once your Schnauzer has learned to fetch an object and bring it on command, you can add *"Give!"* to its vocabulary. This is used to convey that whatever has been fetched should be dropped on the ground at your feet. Again, give a small treat as positive reinforcement for obedient performance.

Carry an Object

The commands *fetch* and *carry* both center around your dog's transporting an object to you by mouth.

Start your instruction by placing rolled newspaper or a nonresinous wooden stick between your dog's jaws. Give the command *"Carry!"* as you do this; if your dog keeps the object in its mouth, praise it. If your Schnauzer immediately drops the object, repeat the command and replace the stick or paper in the dog's mouth. It should not take long to learn this useful trick.

Avoid an Object

A very useful, even lifesaving, command to teach your dog is to refrain from touching an object within grasping range. Dangerous objects, strange food items, food offered by strangers, and other animals' stools are but a few of the things that many dogs will pick up.

Begin your training session with your Schnauzer on its leash and allow the dog to approach a tempting food item placed on the floor. As the dog bends its head down to smell and grasp the food, immediately and forcefully give the command *"No!"*

Staying at Home Alone

The term "separation anxiety" has been applied to the behavior of animals (and humans, too) when they believe they have been abandoned by their loved ones. It is natural for a young dog to form a close attachment to its owner. In the case of dogs, there is the uncertainty of not knowing why they were left alone and when their owner will return. *Consistency* is vital to assure successful training of your dog.

Once your Schnauzer puppy has become accustomed to the concept that your home is its home also, it is appropriate to begin training the dog to stay home alone without misbehaving.

You should start your puppy's training to stay alone by placing it in a small room with one or more of its favorite toys. Calmly close the door to the room, speaking to the puppy as you depart. It will probably try to squeeze out through the doorway, and you must gently, yet firmly, push it back and close the door without slamming it. Remain relaxed and positive. Say *"Good-bye"* as if it were the most natural thing to be leaving the puppy alone.

The Giant Schnauzer has the protective instincts to make anyone feel secure and the essential size and strength to be an effective deterrent to any potential wrongdoer.

If your puppy barks or whines, use a firm voice command of *"No!"* each time it vocalizes.

If your puppy remains quiet for a few minutes, open the door and praise your pet lavishly, conveying to it how happy you are to see it again, but do not overdramatize your return.

Repeat the process of leaving your Schnauzer alone for varying periods of from several minutes to several hours. Each time you return to release it from confinement, go through the ritual of praise. Try to make these periods of confinement as irregular as possible, so that your puppy cannot associate them with your daily schedule. The most important things for your puppy to learn are that you *will* return and that being alone is not a form of punishment.

Chewing on furniture, urination, and defecation while confined to a room are sometimes problems associated with separation anxiety in dogs. With thoughtful and consistent training,

each of these offenses can be eliminated. It is better to learn good habits from the start rather than to retrain an already misbehaving puppy.

Another approach is to confine your puppy to a traveling crate containing a blanket, towel, and a favorite toy for brief periods that lengthen gradually until the puppy grows accustomed to the security of this familiar environment.

Training for Guard Duties

Because all the Schnauzers are so intelligent, they tend to learn readily. It is natural for a dog to protect its home territory from strangers. You probably will not have to actually teach your young dog to be protective, but if you wish to have your dog specifically trained for security work, it is imperative that it first be well versed in simple obedience.

All the Schnauzers excel in Obedience competition. Here a Miniature takes the high jump in style in the demanding Utility class.

As soon as your dog hears your doorbell, it should react to the sound by barking or growling. You should praise your Schnauzer for this quick reaction. If the dog is not already at the door, command it to *"Come!"* and *"Sit!"* Having a family member or friend ring the bell for you while you are in the house with your dog helps this training. At no time should you permit your dog to make actual contact with the "stranger." A sharp bark or two is all that you are aiming for at this point.

If you wish to have your Schnauzer trained to do more than alert you to the presence of strangers, you should consult one or more professional dog trainers for an evaluation of your dog's suitability for more aggressive guard duty.

The Responsible Dog Owner

With fewer people living on farms, ranches, and even in single-family housing, it is no longer socially responsible for a dog owner to allow a pet companion to run free. Today when one's home is shared with a dog, a "social contract" must exist so the dog will not become a nuisance to neighbors.

As citizens of an expanded community, we must assure those with whom we live that they will not be victimized by odor and noise pollution from the presence of our canine companions. Obviously, a dog must never constitute a physical threat to our children and other pets.

In summary, a dog should be an enriching bonus to our life; it must never become a creature that only complicates our daily existence.

This Standard Schnauzer is a trained assistance dog, guiding a deaf owner through a hearing world. The orange vest proclaims to all that this is a dog with a mission.

Housebreaking your new Schnauzer puppy begins as soon as it arrives at your home. Puppies, like human infants, are stimulated to urinate and defecate when they are fed. Knowing this fact will make it easier to train your new dog to carry out these normal bodily functions. The ideal age for housebreaking is probably about 12 to 16 weeks. By then, your puppy will be better able to control its urination and defecation because of the progressive maturation of its body and nervous system. You might have acquired your Schnauzer puppy when it was only 7 to 8 weeks old, however. That is no cause for great concern; with compassionate care and attention to its needs and abilities, housebreaking can still be accomplished with relative ease.

If you live in a house with a yard, take your puppy outside to an area selected by you. If you are an apartment dweller and have no yard in which your puppy can exercise and eliminate, select a small room or an isolated site in one room and cover it with clean newspaper.

Immediately after feeding your puppy or after it awakens, take it either outside or to its special room with the paper-covered area and wait until it urinates, which should not be long.

At first, when the puppy does as expected, it is likely that it was by sheer coincidence. Reach down and give praise while speaking in an encouraging fashion and gently petting it all the time: "What a *good* doggie!"

Praise each good performance lavishly. If, as is quite

normal during the first few days of training, your puppy has an "accident" and fails to visit its assigned toilet spot, place a small amount of its urine on a piece of absorbent cotton or bathroom tissue and deposit it onto the fresh newspaper so that a familiar scent is left. Only a few drops are necessary to achieve the desired effect. When the paper is soiled, remove it and replace it with a fresh supply. Gradually reduce the size of the newspaper-covered floor area until it is only a small spot the size of a large magazine. Before long, your "sure-shot Ulysses" should be able to hit that smaller target with few, if any, misses.

Remember that dogs are unable to read! Your puppy is in the process of being trained to consider paper a surface upon which to deposit its bodily wastes. *If you carelessly leave an important document on the floor unattended, your puppy may perceive it as nothing more than a novel place to use as a toilet!* (The Internal Revenue Service is unlikely to show much sympathy if your puppy used your tax forms as a bathroom fixture.)

If your training is successful, your new Schnauzer puppy should be well on its way to

The basis for clean habits starts in the nest. Nursing puppies will instinctively seek a toilet spot as far as possible from where they eat and sleep.

being housebroken in about a week. Occasional lapses will invariably occur, but these will become uncommon events as the puppy matures and its capacity to retain its urine and stools increases.

Another popular method for housebreaking a naïve puppy is to confine it to a crate or carrier during the training periods following meals. Being fastidious creatures, dogs do not like to soil their dens—in this instance, their crates. Line the crate with fresh newspaper and also put in a soft towel or washable cotton blanket. You can also include one or more of your puppy's favorite chew toys. The metal doors of many of these crates are fitted with food and water containers so that you can feed your puppy in its cage.

Immediately after feeding your puppy, remove it from the crate to relieve itself in its special toileting area. If the puppy mistakenly soils its crate, use a few words of disapproval. *Do not punish it severely or rub its nose in its urine;* that will only confuse the puppy and sow the seeds of future behavioral problems. If you find feces or urine *more* than a few minutes after your puppy defecated or urinated, however, there is no use in even reprimanding the puppy, because it is unlikely that it will associate these deposits with the reason for punishment.

Remember to treat the carrier or crate as a den and thus a site of peaceful refuge, not a place where punishment is administered. After all, you will be using a carrier when traveling with your pet and you should avoid creating any negative associations with the carrier.

Housebreaking is a course of instruction best accomplished with love, not fear! A mild oral reprimand delivered in a stern voice can work wonders because puppies are pack animals and are "programmed" to please their pack leader (you).

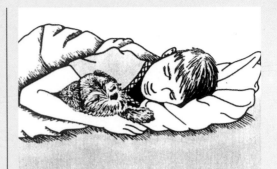

One excellent method for housebreaking a puppy is to recruit a household member to sleep with the newcomer and immediately take it outside at the first sign of waking.

A young puppy, like any other immature creature, has an incompletely developed nervous system; thus, do not expect it to behave in an adult manner, especially in regard to toilet habits (which will be developed after a short time).

Once, when we had just acquired a 6-week-old Schnauzer puppy, we decided to leave the housebreaking chores to our 12-year-old son. We contracted to pay him 10 cents per hour for his efforts. We placed a sleeping bag in our kitchen each evening, and our son and his new companion slept together next to a door leading into our garden. Each time our new puppy stirred in its sleep or got up, our son would arise and take it outdoors. Within a record time of only about three days, our puppy was almost completely housebroken. If your family and living circumstances permit it, you might wish to try this method for your new Schnauzer puppy.

This was the only time that I relented and recommended that our dog sleep with one of us, but (in my opinion) the circumstances—and the results—merited that permissiveness!

IN SICKNESS AND IN HEALTH

Just as humans, dogs have a wide variety of health care needs. Happily we are now better able to meet more of them.

Disease Prevention Measures

We live in an age of veterinary enlightenment where most of the communicable diseases of dogs can be prevented by timely vaccination. Once devastating internal parasitic diseases are now readily controlled by appropriate medication. External parasites such as fleas, ticks, mites, and lice are now easily killed and their reinfestation repelled.

Vaccinations

Preventive vaccination against several infectious canine diseases must be part of your Schnauzer's early life with you. Since the

Your Schnauzer depends on you to provide all its health care needs. It is fortunate for both dogs and their loving owners that modern veterinary science is now able to better protect the well being of all dogs.

antibodies that your puppy acquired from its previously immunized mother slowly diminish, at about eight weeks the puppy may have lost its resistance to common canine infectious diseases. It is always a sad task for me as a veterinarian to inform a dog owner that a puppy has a serious disease that could have been prevented so easily with proper immunization.

It is important to realize that *any* immunization is relative: Successful prophylactic prevention of infectious disease depends upon the immune response to any given vaccine, its dosage and potency, the inherent ability of an individual to mount an increased antibody level, and the virulence or infectivity of any challenging bacterium or virus. It is for these reasons that your veterinarian adheres to a carefully designed vaccination schedule followed with periodic "booster" vaccinations.

The common diseases against which young puppies are routinely immunized are canine distemper, infectious canine hepatitis, canine

Quick Reference Chart for Canine Infectious Diseases

Sign or Symptom	Canine Distemper	Infectious Canine Hepatitis	Parvoviral Gastroenteritis	Coronaviral Gastroenteritis	Parainfluenza	Leptospirosis	Rabies
Vomiting	X	X	X	X		X	
Diarrhea	X	X	X*	X**		X	
"Cold" or "Flu"	X	†		X	X	†	
Convulsions, Seizures, "Fits"	X	†				†	X
Hardening of the Foot and Nose Pads	X						

*The diarrhea seen in cases of parvoviral gastroenteritis often is light-gray, yellow-gray, or hemorrhagic
**The diarrhea seen in coronaviral gastroenteritis often is yellow-orange, occasionally bloody.
†A variable sign in this disease.

parvoviral gastroenteritis, canine coronaviral gastroenteritis, parainfluenza, leptospirosis, and rabies. There are available so-called polyvalent vaccines that contain the immunizing agents for the first six diseases, so that your Schnauzer will have to receive only one broad-scope injection plus another for rabies vaccination.

Canine distemper: Canine distemper is characterized by a large number of signs or symptoms. Early in the disease, the infected dog will exhibit a fever of from 103.5 to 105.5°F (39.8 to 41°C), but the dog's body temperature soon decreases to the normal 100.5 to 102.5°F (38 to 39°C) only to become elevated again in about two days. Typical signs are exhaustion, vomiting, diarrhea, tonsillitis, coughing, mucus-laden dis-

charges from the nose and eyes, hardening of the foot, toe, and nose pads, and central nervous system (brain and spinal cord) disorders ranging from minor nervous tics to major convulsions. Classically, if any four of these signs are seen together, a tentative diagnosis of canine distemper should be considered. Often the affected dog appears to recover from the first signs of gastrointestinal and respiratory disease, only to begin to exhibit signs of severe brain damage about six weeks after the illness first began. The death rate from distemper may be as high as 75 percent. The virus of canine distemper is spread from dog to dog via eating, drinking, or inhaling infective materials in mucous secretions, vomitus, or stools. The virus may be spread by humans that have handled sick dogs shedding the virus. Infective virus may also be carried on the shoes of people who have walked where an infected dog has discharged the contents of its stomach, intestines, or mucus from its lungs.

Dogs should receive yearly booster immunizations for canine distemper.

Adenovirus (Infectious canine hepatitis): The virus of infectious canine hepatitis is not infectious for humans and is unrelated to infectious hepatitis in people.

The physical signs of infectious canine hepatitis are fatigue, tonsillitis, loss of appetite, fever, vomiting, diarrhea, and abdominal pain. Often, if there is substantial liver damage, the whites of the dog's eyes may change to bright yellow. If the dog survives for several weeks, its corneas may become cloudy and milky blue-white; this alteration lasts for a week or so and then slowly returns to normal.

The infectious hepatitis virus is shed in the urine and feces of infected dogs. The death rate may exceed 60 percent in unprotected puppies.

It is general practice to include infectious canine hepatitis vaccine in your dog's annual booster immunization.

Canine parvoviral gastroenteritis: Relatively new to North American dogs, canine parvovirus made its debut as a severe epidemic disease in the late 1970s. In young and adult dogs, parvovirus infection manifests itself in acute fatigue, high fever, profuse vomiting, diarrhea (often bloody), and profound dehydration from the loss of body fluids. In unborn fetuses, the heart muscle is often severely damaged; many puppies born after having contracted parvovirus while in the uterus of the female subsequently die of heart failure.

Canine parvoviral gastroenteritis is spread from an infected dog to a susceptible (nonimmunized) dog by contact with feces, vomitus, or blood. The virus also can be carried on the shoes and clothing of humans exposed to infective material.

Yearly booster vaccinations are recommended; they are usually included in polyvalent vaccines for the major diseases of dogs.

Canine coronaviral gastroenteritis: Superficially very similar in signs and symptoms to canine parvoviral gastroenteritis, this virus disease of young pups usually is substantially milder and less deadly. Some dogs may become severely ill and may even die from this condition, but these are unusual. The major signs of coronavirus infection in puppies and young dogs are a sudden onset of vomiting and diarrhea, loss of appetite, dehydration, and a mild fever. The duration of the disease is seven to ten days. One consistent feature of this disease that helps differentiate it from parvovirus infection is the yellow-orange, occasionally bloody diarrhea.

Parainfluenza: Commonly called "kennel cough" because it causes persistent coughing, infection with canine parainfluenza virus or a combination of parainfluenza and other viruses produce upper and lower respiratory illnesses. Although usually not life-threatening, these disorders are unpleasant for the affected dogs, and because of the almost constant and often protracted coughing, are very annoying for the dogs' owners—and neighbors. The coughing can usually be controlled with anticough medications prescribed by your veterinarian.

Parainfluenza virus is spread from one dog to others by contact of unvaccinated dogs with the coughed-up mucus and other wastes from carrier canines. Humans can also carry the virus on their clothing and shoes.

All dogs love to play in the outdoors; so do many external parasites. Be careful to check your dog after it has been where it might have been exposed to fleas, ticks, or other pests.

Prophylactic immunization with parainfluenza virus vaccine has been shown to be effective in protecting dogs from "kennel cough." Booster vaccination should be given yearly as part of a routine immunization program.

Leptospirosis: Unlike the other prevalent infectious diseases of dogs, which are viral, leptospirosis is a bacterial infection common to many species of mammals, including humans. Ordinarily the leptospiral bacteria are shed in the urine of carrier animals, and infection occurs when susceptible dogs are exposed to that urine. Even dogs that recovered several months earlier from active leptospirosis can continue to act as carriers of the disease to unvaccinated dogs. It is possible for humans to be infected through contact with an infected

dog's urine; strict hygiene is therefore essential when dealing with a proven case of leptospirosis. This includes careful washing of hands, use of disposable food and water bowls, and household bleach disinfection of all surfaces that were in contact with urine, vomitus, or stools.

The signs of the acute phase of leptospirosis may mimic those of both canine distemper and infectious canine hepatitis: fatigue, loss of appetite, fever, tonsillitis, ocular or nasal discharge, vomiting, abdominal pain, and muscular pain. The white portion of the eyes may become yellow, as they do with infectious canine hepatitis, and in severe cases the skin and gums may become yellowish.

With appropriate and aggressive antibiotic and supportive therapy, most dogs infected with the leptospirosis bacteria will recover, but a prolonged period of convalescence may be required before return to full health. Dogs should receive annual booster immunization for leptospirosis.

Rabies: Known from earliest historic times as a menace to humans, rabies remains a justifiably much-feared disease of warm-blooded animals. Many species of wildlife, such as bats, skunks, foxes, raccoons, and feral (wild) cats and dogs serve as natural reservoirs of the virus. Rabies is deadly. Therefore, your dog must be vaccinated at four to six months of age (depending upon the state in which you reside) and every two to three years thereafter. Very effective vaccines have made rabies in properly vaccinated dogs extremely rare. Rabies in dogs may take either of two forms: in the "furious" form, the dog is extremely aggressive and often attacks other animals, humans, or even inanimate objects. In the "dumb" form, the dog becomes extremely lethargic and gradually lapses into torpor. In either case, there is a great tendency for the infected victim to avoid water; hence the common term for the disease, "hydrophobia." One can become infected when the saliva from either form of a rabid animal enters an open skin wound.

Lyme Disease: Although there is a vaccine available for the immunization against canine borreliosis (Lyme Disease), its efficacy and length of protection are, as yet, unclear. In geographical regions known to be heavily tick-infested, and if your Schnauzer is often in wooded areas where ticks abound, the use of this vaccine is probably justified. However, care should also be taken to examine your pet (and yourself) frequently for ticks. Some topical sprays, powders, and flea and tick collars are moderately effective in preventing ticks from attaching themselves to your pet.

Worming

The major gastrointestinal parasites of dogs are roundworms of several species, tapeworms, hookworms, whipworms, *and* some protozoa.

Roundworms: Even the very best kennels encounter the problem of roundworm infestation in puppies that are born from previously dewormed females; this is because some forms of worms exist in tissues other than those of the gastrointestinal tract of the pregnant female and so are unaffected by routine deworming

Always watch your dog to prevent accidental poisoning and learn which plants and flowers carry the potential for harm.

treatments. It is important therefore that all new puppies have their stools examined microscopically for the presence of roundworm eggs. This examination should be repeated at least once more by the time the puppy is ten weeks old, because it may take that long for the immature worms that were transferred to the puppy across the placenta from the female to migrate through the puppy's liver and lungs and eventually reach the intestines. Once present in the stomach and intestines, roundworms may make their presence known by being vomited by the puppy, but if your puppy does not vomit them, you may never know that they are infesting your pet. Ideally, the stools should be rechecked when the puppy reaches 14 weeks of age. Each time the stools are found to be positive for worm eggs that puppy should be properly dewormed with one or more medications called anthelmintics.

Once your Schnauzer is shown to be free of roundworms on two successive stool examinations, it will not have to be dewormed further

Poisonous or Noxious Plants

Listed below is a brief *partial* list of poisonous or noxious plants to which your Schnauzer might be exposed:

African lily	Castor bean	Narcissus
Aloe	Columbine	Oleander
Amaryllis	Common privet	Philodendron
Anemone	Coral plant	Poinsettia
Asparagus fern	Crocus	Potato (sprouted)
Autumn crocus	Croton	Pothos
Azalea	Chinaberry tree	Privet
Baneberry	Chinese lantern	Ranunculus
Belladonna	Christmas cactus	Rhubarb (uncooked)
Bird-of-paradise	Cyclamen	Rosary bean
Bloodroot	Daffodil	Rubber tree
Boston ivy	Hyacinth	Salmonberry
Bottlebrush	Ivy	Snapdragon
Buttercup	Jerusalem cherry	Star of Bethlehem
Caladium	Lantana	Sweet pea
Calla lily	Lily of the valley	Taro
Mushrooms (some)	Mistletoe	Tulip

unless it becomes reinfested by ingesting worm eggs from an infected environment.

Tapeworms: Ribbonlike tapeworm segments called *proglottids* are sometimes seen either on the surfaces of your dog's formed stools or crawling from its anus. Soon after they are exposed to air, these segments become desiccated, shrink, and look like grains of rice.

The most common species of tapeworms affecting urban dogs is *Dipylidium caninum,* which requires a common dog flea as its intermediate host. The larval fleas ingest eggs that are enclosed within the proglottids, and intermediate stages of the tapeworms soon develop within the fleas' bodies. Soon after being ingested by a dog as it grooms itself, the infected fleas release the immature tapeworms into the digestive canal of the dog; there the immature tapeworms become adults and complete their life cycle by producing more eggs.

Other species of tapeworms may infest your Schnauzer. Some utilize small rodents and rabbits as intermediate hosts, and at least one tapeworm species affecting dogs uses sheep and deer as hosts.

Several excellent antitapeworm medications are available from your family veterinarian. Because of their life cycles and physiological characteristics, tapeworms are not effectively treated by medications for roundworms.

To keep your Schnauzer free from tapeworms, it is essential that it also be kept free from fleas.

Hookworms: Hookworms, like roundworms, can be transmitted from an infected mother dog to her unborn puppies. The tiny immature worms travel across the placental membranes from which the fetal puppies are nourished. Unlike roundworms, hookworms can kill young dogs rapidly. Infestation often results in severe anemia within only a few weeks of birth. Older dogs also can become infested when they ingest infected material deposited by another animal, or by walking upon moist soil contaminated by infective immature hookworm larvae.

Hookworm infestation is diagnosed by microscopic examination of your Schnauzer puppy's stools. If your puppy is shown to be infested, it must be effectively treated by an appropriate medication dispensed by your veterinarian. To avoid becoming infested, you and other members of your household should wash your hands carefully after handling your dog.

Whipworms: Although they are not encountered as commonly as the other forms of worms mentioned, whipworms also can be a problem with pet dogs. These parasites usually take up residence in your dog's cecum, the blind pouchlike counterpart of the human vermiform appendix; here they often cause considerable inflammation and discomfort. An infested dog often bites and chews at its flank in attempts to ease its pain.

Diagnosis of whipworm infestation is made by finding the characteristic eggs in the stools of infected dogs.

Because of their preference for the cecum, whipworms can be difficult to treat, but today several new drugs have proved effective.

Heartworms: Although it does not infest the gastrointestinal tracts of dogs, the heartworm, *Dirofilaria immitis,* nevertheless is a significant parasite of dogs in many areas of North America. The life cycle of the heartworm requires one of several species of mosquito. Adult heartworms reside in the chambers of the heart and pulmonary vessels. There they mate, and as the young worms, called *microfilaria,* are released into the bloodstream, they are ingested with the blood that female mosquitoes must have before they can produce eggs. The microfilaria are then injected into dogs bitten by the infected mosquitoes.

Although treatment to rid an infested dog of its adult heartworms is possible, it entails the use of toxic drugs that must be administered only under controlled conditions by a veterinarian experienced in this treatment.

Rather than placing the major emphasis on treatment, veterinarians now recommend prevention of infection with microfilaria by giving dogs who live in or travel through heartworm-endemic areas a specific medication called diethylcarbamazine. This very effective drug is sold under a variety of trade names. The drug is given daily, usually as a palatable tablet that most dogs will accept as a treat. This drug must be given only to dogs that have been shown on laboratory examination of their blood to be *free* from microfilariae and, thus by infestation with adult heartworms. If your Schnauzer is found to be infested already, it must NOT be treated with diethylcarbamazine. The yearly cost for protecting a Giant or Standard Schnauzer is approximately 35 to 40 dollars; for a Miniature Schnauzer, the cost is approximately 18 to 24 dollars, depending upon the weight of each dog and the brand of product used.

Flea and Tick Control

Like other breeds of dogs, Schnauzers can serve as unwilling hosts to fleas and ticks. Not being very discriminating in their choice of victims, these unpleasant parasites also can bite humans.

Fortunately, there is a wide variety of excellent flea and tick sprays and powders available from veterinarians and some pet suppliers. Many of these products not only kill the fleas and ticks, but also repel reinfestation. If you experience a flea or tick problem, one or more of these products should be used routinely and according to the package instructions. Where appropriate, you should spray your premises to eradicate breeding populations of these parasites in your household.

Specific skin conditions related to flea infestation are discussed in the section Disorders of the Coat and Skin (see page 82).

Procedures You Should Master

Giving Medications

Tablets and capsules: While you speak gently and confidently to your Schnauzer, hold its muzzle with your nondominant hand and elevate its head to about a 45-degree angle. With your dominant hand, use your finger to open the jaw by pushing down on the central teeth.

Place the tablet or capsule over the back of the tongue, as far as you can. Remove your fingers, close the dog's mouth, and stroke its neck or rub its nose vigorously. In some instances, some pills and capsules can be hidden in a small amount of the dog's favorite food. Alternatively, the contents of some capsules may be mixed with food; this technique is not appropriate with medications that have a bad taste. Giving the medication directly is usually most effective.

Liquid medications: Tip you Schnauzer's head back slightly with your nondominant hand. With the third finger of your dominant hand, open the jaw by pushing down on the lower central teeth. Using a plastic *(NOT GLASS)* eyedropper or metal spoon, place the required amount of liquid medication over the back of the tongue or into the dog's cheek. Close the mouth, and rub your pet's nose pad vigorously; this last maneuver will induce the dog to swallow and lick its nose. Before you release your Schnauzer, praise it lavishly for its fine cooperation.

Obtaining Your Dog's Pulse

The pulse beat of your dog is most conveniently found on the inner aspect of either hind leg, a few inches above the knee joint. As you feel the inside of the leg at this point, you will find a shallow groove in which the large femoral artery and vein lie. With gentle pressure from your fingertip you will feel the arterial pulse that corresponds to each contraction of your dog's

Administering a tablet or capsule. The medication is placed as far back as possible over your dog's tongue, the mouth is closed, and the nose pad is briskly rubbed to induce swallowing.

left ventricle. Using a watch, time the number of pulse beats for 15 or 30 seconds and multiply the number of beats by either four or two, as appropriate, to know the pulse rate per minute.

Restraining Your Dog

When walking your Schnauzer on crowded city streets or when taking it to the veterinarian, you should always restrain it with a proper leash attached to its collar. You may encounter other dogs on the street; having your companion properly leashed will prevent tragic accidents. At the veterinary hospital other pet owners may be in the reception area; having each animal controlled on a leash or confined to a carrier will be appreciated and will make everyone's visit safe and more enjoyable.

If your Schnauzer is an intact female and if she is in heat, it is only courteous and proper that you do not walk her in the neighborhood until her estrus period is completed.

To Spay or Not to Spay

The foremost advantage to spaying a female puppy is that it will render her permanently sterile. After the surgical removal of your female's ovaries and uterus, she will no longer experience estrous cycling, which is often inconvenient. We know that if a female is spayed before her first estrus, it is very unlikely that she will develop malignant breast tumors; any mammary tumors will almost always be benign. Of course, the possibility of any ovarian and uterine problems will be eliminated. Also, most vaginal disorders will be avoided.

If the spay operation is performed before the female's onset of sexual maturity, the female will be far less likely to become obese—unless

CHECKLIST

Spaying and Neutering

Some gender-specific disadvantages can be avoided by spaying a female dog or neutering a male dog (these are surgical sterilization operations performed by veterinarians). Show dogs are not spayed or neutered because altered dogs cannot be shown in conformation shows. I strongly recommend that your pet Schnauzer be spayed or neutered.

✔ Spaying or neutering will not change your pet's personality or induce obesity, unless you feed it too much or fail to exercise it sufficiently.

✔ Spaying or neutering confers significant health benefits, such as decreasing the incidence of mammary (breast) tumors in females, and testicular- and prostate-related disorders in males.

✔ Spayed or neutered dogs usually stay close to home. Because they tend to wander less than intact dogs, they are less likely to be exposed to automobile accidents and other dogs with communicable diseases, or to engage in fights with vicious dogs.

✔ By having your Schnauzer spayed or neutered, you will help reduce the number of unwanted dogs in this country.

you or other family members grossly overfeed her. A female puppy that is spayed early usually will retain her playfulness well into her later years. Data now suggests that the spayed female lives a longer and healthier life, particularly after her tenth year of age.

The *only* disadvantage to spaying a female is the loss of her fertility. The popular belief that spaying makes a female into a fat, lazy, lackluster, and personality-flawed creature is simply not true. As has been observed by ALPO Pet Center, "There are no fat dogs . . . just overfed dogs!"

A male dog neutered when it is between 10 to 12 months of age already will have learned to "hike" its leg when it urinates and most likely will not have acquired most of the mature sexual behavior characteristics that develop during its second year of life. If neutered early in life, a male dog is much less likely to become obese or lose any of its positive personality traits.

Because several diseases of male dogs are so closely related to the influence of male sex hormones, the neutered male dog will escape many of the disorders of the aging intact male, such as testicular and scrotal tumors, perineal hernias, and perianal gland tumors.

From the immediate practical standpoint, the greatest benefit to neutering a male dog is that once the source of male hormones is removed, the socially unacceptable sexual behavior that many house or apartment-raised intact dogs display is *prevented.* This is particularly true in the case of males that are sexually naïve at the time that they are neutered.

Generally, male dogs that have been neutered early in their young adult life retain their splendid personalities and do not grow obese. The neutered dog tends to display somewhat less aggressiveness toward other dogs and is much less likely to engage in dog-fights. Research has shown that neutered male dogs live longer than intact males.

For all these valid reasons male guide dogs for the blind are routinely neutered.

Aside from permanent sterilization, there are no disadvantages to this procedure.

Diseases and Disorders

Diabetes

Many people do not realize that dogs and other animals can develop diabetes. Similar to the physical effects and symptoms in humans, diabetes mellitus ("sugar" diabetes) manifests itself in dogs by weight loss, increased appetite and thirst, increased urinary output, an odor of acetone on the breath, and decreased ability to fight infections. Later, in the untreated or ineffectively treated diabetic dog, the eyesight and vascular system may become severely affected, leading to blindness, vascular insufficiency, and kidney disease.

Success in managing a diabetic dog takes a team effort. Your veterinarian can help establish a proper diet and the correct dosage of insulin; you will be responsible for many daily details, so that your dog's dietary intake remains constant *and* its urine and blood glucose are monitored regularly. After a few weeks, you and your veterinarian will have established a daily treatment regimen that will maintain your Schnauzer's health. A properly treated diabetic dog should enjoy a satisfactory life for many years after the initial diagnosis of its disease.

Tonsillitis

Many people are surprised to learn that dogs possess tonsils. Sometimes these paired lymph-node-like organs in the back of a dog's throat become inflamed and greatly enlarged. Affected dogs may lose their appetites because of a sore throat, salivate excessively, and/or develop soft, dry coughs.

Often the inflamed tonsils respond quickly to appropriate antibiotic therapy. Sometimes, if your dog has experienced recurrent or chronic tonsillitis, your veterinarian may recommend surgical removal of the tonsils. This operation is relatively minor, with low risk of complications. A bland, soft diet is fed for a day or two after the tonsillectomy; recovery is usually quite rapid.

Epilepsy

Dogs sometimes develop epilepsy. The causes for this brain disorder are unclear, but some breeds of dogs are known to experience epileptiform seizures more often than other breeds. In some cases, trauma to the head has been implicated; in others, inadequate oxygen to the fetus during its passage through the birth canal has been suggested. Still other cases of epilepsy are associated with brain tumors, abscesses, or migrating parasites.

Some forms of epilepsy are seen in young puppies, but more typically, the seizure disorder is observed for the first time in fully grown dogs. The two main categories of epileptiform seizures are *grand mal* and *petit mal.* In a grand mal seizure, the affected dog usually loses consciousness, may thrash its legs, clamp its jaws tightly shut, and salivate profusely. Urine and/or feces may be released during the seizure. The duration of such an event is usually less than two minutes. In a petit mal seizure, the dog usually does not lose consciousness and may appear to be only momentarily stuporous.

A dog who displays a seizure disorder should be examined by a veterinarian. There are some very effective oral medications to control this condition. Many epileptic dogs can live out full and satisfactory life spans.

Kidney Diseases

Prevention: The vast majority of dogs live their entire lives without developing significant kidney disease. Because one of the major causes for kidney disease is leptospirosis, it is important that your Schnauzer be kept current in its routine booster vaccinations.

The water you offer your dog must always be clean, fresh, and available at all times. The important kidney tissues can be damaged by prolonged and chronic lack of water.

Dogs require food containing high-quality protein, but the quantity should not be excessive; young puppies require a somewhat higher protein level because they must make body tissues during this rapid growth phase; adult dogs need only maintain body tissues. Foods with very high protein content can abnormally burden the kidneys.

Some common household chemicals can severely damage kidney tissues. Automobile antifreeze solution containing ethylene glycol is an example of such an agent. By simply storing antifreeze safely and discarding it properly, much poisoning can be avoided. Some heavy metals that are common ingredients of insecticides also are toxic to the kidneys. Some dogs, if given the opportunity, will drink or each such products. Here again, prevention is the best medicine. Excessive salt in the diet also can damage the kidneys.

Some plants contain toxic elements that can adversely affect kidney function. It is beyond the scope of this guidebook to enumerate these plant species, but if you find your dog chewing your houseplants, take action immediately;

correct your dog's misbehavior, eliminate the particular plants, or place them where your dog can no longer reach them.

Maintenance of dogs with chronic kidney dysfunction: For whatever reason your Schnauzer develops kidney disease, there are simple things that you can do that will greatly reduce the burden of work on the kidneys. Numerous special high-quality/low-quantity protein commercial products are available from your veterinarian. Alternatively, there are several excellent recipes for homemade diets for canine kidney patients. Most of these recipes are based on rice, cottage cheese, boiled chicken, and tofu (soybean cake), to which you add vitamins and low-sodium or sodium-free condiments for palatability. Your family veterinarian can help you with the choice of diet to match your dog's requirements.

Because a dog with kidney disease often cannot concentrate its urine normally, a ready source of fresh water is absolutely essential. Your kidney-deficient Schnauzer must *never* be deprived of water.

Properly managed, dogs with even moderate kidney dysfunction can live several years after their disease was diagnosed.

Because of its lack of urine concentration and the consequently greater urine volume produced daily, your dog may find it difficult to maintain its previous faultless housebroken behavior. A free-swinging "doggie door" will provide a ready exit to a backyard or run to facilitate your dog's elimination outdoors.

Urinary Bladder Disorders

Cystitis: Dogs, like humans, occasionally develop inflammation of the urinary bladder. The medical term for this disorder is *cystitis.*

The major clinical signs of cystitis are frequent urination and blood in the urine. Your veterinarian may employ special X-ray techniques in making the diagnosis and probably will prescribe specific antibiotics for its treatment. Often an increased water intake will aid in the therapy by diluting the total volume of urine. A small increase in dietary salt, as sodium chloride, may help, but be certain that you obtain your veterinarian's advice on this. If the dog will drink it, cranberry juice may help, because it increases the urine's acidity.

Bladder and urethral stones: Dogs, like humans, sometimes develop urinary bladder and urethral stones. Some dog breeds have their own characteristic types of chemical stones. Fortunately, the Giant, Standard, and Miniature Schnauzers are not particularly prone to stone formation.

Urinary stones or "calculi" can, if they obstruct the outflow of urine, lead to severe retention, pain, and eventual death. More commonly, bladder stones remain in the body of the bladder; the stones induce an inflammation that often leads to bleeding. The first sign that you may note is the presence of blood-tinged urine. Often the affected dog urinates more frequently than normal. Abdominal X rays will confirm your veterinarian's tentative diagnosis. Most urinary bladder stones require surgical removal. The surgery is usually not especially difficult and generally you can expect an uneventful recovery. Your veterinarian should have the stone(s) analyzed, so that if a dietary change is necessary, one can be prescribed.

The urethra is the narrow tube that conducts urine from the bladder to the outside of the body. Stones that become lodged in the urethra require immediate veterinary medical and surgi-

Every dog should have an annual veterinary examination. Consider it insurance for your dog's health and welfare.

cal intervention. These stones are usually small and enter the urethra from the urinary bladder, where they were formed earlier. The stones usually progress down the urethra until they reach a location where the narrow diameter will not permit further passage.

There are some nonsurgical medical measures that your veterinarian may employ to try to dislodge urethral stones, but you should be prepared for the possibility that surgery may be necessary to remove them.

Once the stones are removed, your veterinarian will send them to a laboratory for chemical analysis. When the analysis is known, your veterinarian will advise you to alter your dog's diet to reduce the possibility of further stone formation and a recurrence of obstruction.

Disorders of the Male Reproductive Tract

Testicular tumors: Tumors of the canine testicles are commonly encountered in veterinary medical practice. Most of these growths are seen in dogs of at least middle age; the tumors occur with greatest frequency in dogs of 11 to 14 years old. This disorder is rare in young males, although there is one type that specifically affects very young dogs.

Many testicular tumors are first discovered by your family veterinarian during your dog's annual physical examination and booster vaccinations.

Generally, the treatment of choice is to surgically remove the testicle in which the tumor is growing. Ideally, the tissue is submitted for microscopic examination by a veterinary pathologist to ascertain whether the tumor was malignant or benign.

By the age at which most of these masses affect dogs, the loss of one—or both—testicles should not result in significant behavioral changes in your pet.

Prostate disorders: The dog is one of the few domestic animals in which prostate disease is common. This is because 1) the dog possesses a prostate gland, much like that of human males, and 2) dogs live long enough for tumors to develop.

Because the prostate gland is dependent upon male hormones secreted by the testicles, prostate disorders, particularly cancer, are almost always confined to intact, nonneutered dogs. As the intact dog ages, there is a marked tendency for the prostate gland, which is located just behind the neck of the urinary bladder, to become enlarged. Affected dogs may experience difficulty when passing their urine or feces. Usually this prostatic enlargement is unrelated to tumor growth, although tumors may arise in the organ.

The prostate occasionally becomes infected and may even develop abscesses that are painful to the dog, especially when it strains to have a bowel movement.

Simple benign prostatic enlargement is often treated by either castration or female hormone (estrogen) therapy. From my point of view as a veterinary surgeon, castration is the preferred treatment, because it is accompanied by the fewest and mildest secondary effects. Similarly, the medical and surgical management of prostatic infections often includes neutering.

Two disorders related to the canine prostate are perineal hernia and perianal gland tumors. Castration is a standard part of the treatment by which each of these conditions is corrected.

From the foregoing discussion, you can see why most veterinary surgeons recommend neutering male dogs early in life; this simple procedure assures the owner that this pet, though sterile, will live a far healthier life than his intact kin.

Disorders of the scrotum: Because it is covered with sensitive skin, the canine scrotum occasionally becomes inflamed when the dog sits on or in an irritating substance, becomes sunburned, or infected. Under most circumstances, the inflamed skin can be treated with soothing anti-inflammatory topical ointments, creams, or lotions prescribed by a veterinarian.

Scrotal tumors are seen in older dogs, but they are not particularly common. Some of these tumors are thought to result from exposure to environmental carcinogens, such as certain chemicals. If the disease is identified early, surgery usually is effective.

Disorders of the penis and prepuce: Because dogs are not circumcised, their penises remain moist at all times. Often this moist and warm environment becomes inflamed and infected with common bacteria, resulting in a chronic discharge. This relatively minor but annoying condition is called *balanoposthitis*. The more your dog licks his organ, the more organisms will gain entrance to this optimal site in which bacteria, yeasts, and fungi flourish. Sometimes a discharge signals the presence of one or more foreign bodies that have gained entrance to the penile sheath, called the prepuce. These foreign bodies can be bristly hairs or barbed-awned weedy plant seeds, called "foxtails."

Your veterinarian should be consulted if you notice a discharge from your dog's prepuce. Various solutions to this unpleasant condition exist, and you can adopt one which is most appropriate for you and your male Schnauzer.

Sometimes a dog will injure its prepuce and/or penis when he jumps over a fence. The prepuce is easily lacerated in this way. If you notice that the skin is traumatized, consult your veterinarian.

Disorders of the Female Reproductive Tract

Intact females may develop the identical diseases that women sometimes develop: ovarian infections, cysts, and tumors; oviductal infections, cysts, and tumors; uterine infections and tumors; vaginal infections and tumors; and other miscellaneous conditions. Of course, most of these maladies can be prevented by having your female spayed early in life.

Ovarian disorders: Ovarian tumors are not rare in females and usually make their presence known by inducing abnormal behavior and/or physical signs of irregular estrus cycling. Some tumors can reach enormous size and become known because of abdominal swelling. I once operated upon a German Shepherd female whose left ovary weighed over fourteen pounds! Some of these masses can be seen or felt as firm, usually round protrusions within your female's abdomen and are discovered when you stroke or examine your pet. Your family veterinarian should be consulted if you find *any* such lump or mass.

Ovarian and oviductal infections are less common. When they are present, the signs and symptoms are abdominal pain, fever, and sterility.

Uterine disorders: The most common disorder of the canine female reproductive tract is uterine infection, called *pyometritis* or *pyometra*. Often the uterine "horns" and body fill with pus, which, because the cervix is closed, cannot drain through the vaginal canal. At other times, the cervix opens and the exudate formed within the uterus drains as a thick, often foul-smelling discharge from the vagina. In either case, affected females may exhibit fever, lethargy, lack of appetite, abdominal distention, and greatly increased thirst. There is always the potential danger that the diseased uterus will rupture into the abdomen and cause severe peritonitis. If you suspect that your female has a uterine infection, you should have her examined immediately.

Although there are some nonsurgical methods for treating uterine infections, most of the cases will eventually require a total removal of the ovaries and uterus. Moreover, once a female has suffered a severe uterine infection, her potential fertility often is substantially reduced.

Uterine tumors are less common, but they are encountered in veterinary surgical practice. Most of these tumors are benign, but a few are found to be malignant.

Examining the superficial parts of the ear.

Vaginal disorders: Infections, cysts, tumors, protrusions, and foreign bodies are some of the more common ailments affecting the canine vagina. Many signal their presence by discharges. Some intact females will exhibit protrusions of the lining of the vagina during the height of their estrus phase of the estrus cycle. Although alarming to the observer, these protrusions will spontaneously regress after ovulation. Once this condition occurs during one estrus, it is common for it to recur during subsequent cycles.

In some areas of the United States, wild grasses abound and their awned seeds can gain entrance to the vagina. These elongated seeds have barbed outer seed coats that cause them to travel in a forward direction only; because these seeds have such sharply pointed ends, they can actually penetrate the tough walls of the vagina and enter the abdominal cavity or migrate to other anatomic sites where they cause severe infections. Often surgery is required to remove the foreign body.

Disorders of the Ear

Infections: Ear infections caused by bacteria, yeasts, and other fungi are most often, but not invariably, encountered in dogs with long and

pendant ear flaps. Even Schnauzers with uncropped ear flaps tend to carry their ears high enough to permit adequate air circulation into and out of the deeper ear canal structures.

Most often, ear infections manifest themselves by foul-smelling discharges, pain that is indicated by your dog's pawing at its ear, and vocalizing with cries or moans. These same signs may suggest that a foreign body has entered the ear canal.

Have your Schnauzer examined by a veterinarian if you suspect an ear infection. Be prepared to allow your pet to be anesthetized while its ears are thoroughly examined, cleansed, and medicated. Often the ears may be so painful that the affected dog will not permit a veterinarian to examine and treat the problem properly unless anesthesia is employed.

Foreign bodies: Foreign bodies can easily enter the ear canal as your dog runs or walks through tall wild grass or weeds whose seeds are protected by tough barbed outer coats called awns. To examine the interior of the ear canal the veterinarian will insert an otoscope, an illuminated instrument fitted with a cone-like speculum. Quite often because of the acute pain that some foreign bodies can produce, your dog will not permit this procedure, and it will have to be briefly anesthetized. If a foreign body is found during this inspection, a special long forceps is used to grasp and withdraw the offending object from the canal. After the ear canals are free of foreign matter, they are cleaned and medicated with anti-inflammatory and antibiotic ointment.

Aural hematomas ("blood blisters"): Sometimes a dog will shake its ears so vigorously that it will sustain an injury to one or more of the blood vessels between the layers of tissue that cover the cartilaginous tissue of the flap. When this happens, the blood escapes from the damaged vessel and creates a large blood "blister," called a hematoma. Usually these hematomas are relatively painless after the initial injury, but are cosmetically unacceptable. Moreover, if not drained, the hematoma will eventually shrink and cause the affected ear flap to become deformed, creating a "cauliflower" ear.

The treatment of choice for these ear flap hematomas is surgical correction. Your veterinarian may advise you to wait for surgery 48 to 72 hours after the initial injury. This will allow the bleeding into the hematoma to cease and the firm clot to form.

At the time of surgery, your veterinarian also will examine your Schnauzer's ear canals to determine the cause for the head shaking that initiated the hematoma and then treat it.

If the surgery is correctly performed, the postsurgical cosmetic appearance of an ear-flap hematoma is quite acceptable.

Ear mites and ticks: Unless your Schnauzer lives with a cat whose ears are infested with ear mites, or has access to wilderness areas where ear ticks abound, it is unlikely to suffer from these highly selective parasites that are distant cousins to spiders.

The signs of ear-mite or tick infestation are pawing at the ear, head shaking, and the presence of a dark, semi-dry, often profuse discharge within the ear canal.

Treatment for ear-mite infestation is thorough cleansing of the ear canals followed by the instillation of an ointment or aqueous solution that will eradicate any mites or their eggs.

Ear ticks are physically removed with forceps inserted through an illuminated ear speculum and otoscope. Once the adult ticks are removed, ear-mite medication is placed into the ear canals to destroy any eggs or larval ticks.

Deafness: It is entirely normal for an aging dog to lose some of its hearing as the years pass. If your young Schnauzer appears to be growing deaf, you should have it examined by a veterinarian; the cause may be as simple as an accumulation of ear wax obstructing the ear canals adjacent to the eardrum. Foreign bodies and tumors are other causes for temporary deafness.

Disorders of the Eye

Injuries: Traumatic injuries to your dog's eyes usually result from objects in the environment such as sticks, weed seeds, and cat-claw scratches. Less commonly, a dog's eyes accidentally may be exposed to caustic or irritating household or garden chemicals. The dog's own paws and claws also can injure the delicate eye and lid tissues as the animal rubs its face.

The major signs of eye injury are pain and excessive secretion of tears. The dog will usually keep its eyelid closed tightly over the injured or inflamed eye.

If you know for certain that some object or chemical irritant entered your pet's eyes, immediately flush the eyes with warm water or, if you have it in your medicine cabinet, a sterile ophthalmic irrigating solution. A good substitute for this product is a hard contact lens wetting solution. Gently open the dog's eyelids by spreading them between the fingers of one hand and then instill or direct a fine stream of irrigating solution onto the cornea. As soon as possible, take your Schnauzer to a veterinarian for examination and evaluation of the extent of injury.

Foreign bodies: If you can see a foreign object protruding from between your dog's eyelids do not attempt to remove it yourself. Many weed seeds have sharply barbed awns and seed coats that can severely lacerate an otherwise undamaged cornea. Your family veterinarian can skillfully extract these objects without creating further trauma, and then the tissues can be examined with special staining techniques to reveal the extent of any damage.

Canine infectious hepatitis–related corneal changes: A frequent sequel to infection with the virus of infectious canine hepatitis is a sudden loss of clarity in one or both corneas. The corneas become milky-blue. Even without therapy this cloudiness usually will clear within a few days. Your veterinarian can prescribe medication that will hasten this clearing.

Cataracts: The loss of clarity in the crystalline lens of the eye is called a cataract.

Normally, the substance of the crystalline lens is absolutely clear, and light passes unimpeded through the lens, to be focused on the retina at the back of the eye. Two major types of cataracts are known: juvenile and mature. The juvenile form usually occurs rather suddenly and prior to the eighth year of life. The mature form develops much more slowly and is usually seen in dogs at least nine or ten years old.

It is unusual for Schnauzers to develop juvenile cataracts, but if they are seen, you should have your dog examined by a veterinarian skilled in the treatment of eye diseases.

Unless there are secondary changes within the eyes, such as glaucoma, little need be done to treat mature cataracts. They are only a consequence of the gracefully aging elderly dog!

Glaucoma: Glaucoma is defined as an abnormal increase of pressure within the eye. Each normal eye must have a fluid pressure slightly higher than that of the atmosphere, to maintain the internal structures in their normal locations within the globelike eye. The fluid is normally secreted by specialized tissues within the eyes. If anything acts to block the normal drainage of fluid from the eye, the pressure within that eye will increase. Then the eye will enlarge to accommodate the increased fluid volume and pressure. As this happens, delicate nerve tissues can suffer irreparable damage, and total blindness can ensue.

Glaucoma can be either acute, in that its onset is sudden, or gradual, and chronic. The result is the same, but whereas the chronic form is painless, the acute form can be very painful.

An ophthalmologic examination should be part of each annual physical examination of your Schnauzer at the time of its routine booster immunizations. These visits also give you an opportunity to discuss specific questions with your family veterinarian. There is no substitute for sound preventive medicine, for it not only can improve the chances for your loved pet to live to its maximal age in health, but also will certainly save you money.

Disorders of the Coat and Skin

Flea-bite allergy: One of the most frequent disorders of the skin of dogs is allergy to flea saliva that is injected into the skin at the time that the fleas take their blood meals. Many dogs respond to this potent protein allergin by making specific antibodies to it. Within a variable period of time, each new flea bite prompts an intense reaction of local irritation and itching. Sometimes an affected dog will mutilate its own skin by trying to relieve the discomfort. In these instances, a short course of anti-inflammatory cortisone injections or tablets may be indicated to afford your dog temporary relief and allow its skin to heal.

The simplest method for avoiding flea-bite allergy dermatitis is to routinely use a high-quality flea and tick spray or powder. In severe cases of this skin disorder, a single flea bite can arouse an intense allergic reaction. In such a case, your veterinarian may wish to employ a course of desensitizing injections with one of several flea extracts.

Contact dermatitis: There are some substances in the home and outdoor environment to which some dogs acquire an allergic sensitivity; wool carpeting, certain plant fibers, pollens, soaps, and chemical cleansers are examples of such materials.

The symptoms of contact dermatitis in the dog are the same as those seen in humans exposed to poison ivy, oak, and sumac. After the skin has been sensitized by previous exposure, subsequent contact with the allergin will result in an often intense reaction marked by redness, swelling, and itchiness.

To treat this form of allergy, gently wash the skin to remove any residual allergin, then apply soothing lotion containing cortisone or cortisonelike medication. In severe cases, your veterinarian can inject cortisone for quicker relief of the allergic reaction.

Food allergy–related dermatitis: Some dogs develop an allergy to some food items. Milk products, eggs, poultry, meat products, pork, fish, and other seafood are most often implicated in these allergic reactions. The effects of allergy to certain foods may be almost immediately apparent: breathing difficulties, skin rashes ("hives"), excessive secretion of tears and saliva. In a few dogs, the reaction may prove fatal, but these cases usually have had a previous history of acute illness after eating certain foods. Most cases of food allergy dermatitis end spontaneously; others may need the use of antihistamines, cortisonelike drugs, or adrenaline to abolish the signs and symptoms of the acute reaction.

Skin tumors: Tumors of the skin are commonly seen in dogs; some breeds are more prone to developing these lesions than others. The majority of skin tumors in dogs are benign. They may be solitary or multiple, slow growing or rapidly spreading, pigmented or pigment-free. Others are highly malignant and behave aggressively. Some skin tumors are found when dogs are groomed; when the fur is clipped, the previously hidden lesions may be scraped and begin to bleed.

If you discover one or more skin tumors on your Schnauzer, take your pet to its veterinarian for an evaluation and surgical removal, if appro-

priate. The ideal time for surgery is when the skin tumors are still small, because they are most easily removed and leave only small scars; however, even large, broad-based tumors can be removed. It is standard practice to submit each suspected tumor to a pathologist for a diagnosis of its type and potential for aggressive behavior.

Sometimes tumors arise in the fatty tissues just beneath the skin. These masses may be solitary or multiple and usually can be moved freely as the skin is slipped back and forth over them. Most often, these tumors are of fatty origin and are called lipomas. The overwhelming majority are benign and can be removed easily by a veterinary surgeon. Most often, this type of tumor occurs in dogs who are at least middle-aged.

Disorders of the Anal Sacs

Preventing problems: The secretions of the paired anal sacs are employed to scent mark a dog's territory and, to a lesser extent, to help lubricate the anal canal during passage of stools. Each time the dog defecates, there is a little secretion from these twin saclike structures that lie beneath the skin covering the anal sphincter. If a dog is obese, the sacs move into the soft fatty tissue and return after the stools are passed; if the anal sac secretions are thus not released, they often become dried. After a variable period of time, this dried material becomes impacted, and the sac becomes inflamed. Dogs with impacted or irritated anal sacs will "scoot" on their rumps to help relieve their discomfort.

One of the easiest means for preventing anal sac problems is to keep your Schnauzer from becoming obese.

Impaction and abscesses: If you notice that your Schnauzer is experiencing anal sac discomfort, consult your veterinarian for evaluation

Disorders of the Perianal or Circumanal Glands

Dogs possess small perianal or circumanal glands that lie just beneath the skin of the anus. These are separate and distinct from the paired anal sacs. Occasionally these structures become infected or involved in tumor formation.

Infections: Abscesses and fistulas (abnormal passages from an abscess or organ) may develop in these glands; they are troublesome to treat effectively because this region of the body is hardly conducive to strict hygiene.

Home treatment employing the application of hot compresses and antibiotic and anti-inflammatory ointments may be all that is necessary, but more often surgical intervention is required. Your family veterinarian should be consulted for a professional evaluation.

Tumors: Perianal gland tumors are much more common than are abscesses and fistulas. There is evidence today that in the male dog, male hormone, which is secreted by the testicles, tends to foster the growth of these tumors, and therefore they are encountered much more in the male than in the female. If your intact male Schnauzer develops a perianal gland tumor, your veterinarian may advise that you authorize castration of your pet at the time of its anal surgery. In most cases, this is entirely warranted.

Some perianal gland tumors are benign and others are aggressively malignant. Because some otherwise benign tumors are characterized by small clusters of malignant cells, these

and treatment. Because of their closeness to the anus, the anal sacs may become infected with a variety of bacterial organisms and form painful abscesses (inflamed tissue with accumulated pus). An abscessed anal sac may form a draining opening to the outside.

Treatment of impacted or abscessed anal sacs: Often these sacs can be drained and treated with anti-inflammatory ointments and antibiotic injections. A gloved finger is inserted into the anus and each sac is drained separately. This procedure is most effectively performed by a veterinarian. In chronic or severe cases of anal saculitis, your veterinarian may advise the surgical removal of both of these nonessential organs. Once the anal sacs are removed, you will find that your dog will have lost much of its previous "doggy" odor. Some people elect to prevent problems by having their dogs' anal sacs removed at the time of a spay or neutering operation, thus requiring that the animal be anesthetized only once.

tumors should be removed early and examined thoroughly by a veterinary pathologist.

In some very aggressive perianal gland tumors, surgery may not be enough, and radiation therapy is indicated. Fortunately, this tumor type is rather responsive to radiation, and the posttreatment course of recovery is usually satisfactory.

Dental Care

The importance of oral hygiene: In nature, dogs, like their wild cousins, keep their teeth and gums healthy by using them to catch and chew their food. The diets we feed our dogs frequently are insufficiently complex or chewy to furnish much gum and jaw exercise or natural teeth cleaning.

Most dental disease begins with periodontal, or gum deterioration. The previously sound, well-rooted teeth become loosened, abscessed, and eventually fall out of their sockets. The underlying jawbones may become seriously infected. One effect of chronic dental disease may surprise you: as bacteria gain entrance to the vascular system, they may "seed" distant organs with infective material. One of the most common sites for this secondary involvement is the heart valves that direct the flow of blood to and from the heart and lungs. For some reason, this disease, called vegetative endocarditis, is most often observed in the hearts of toy and miniature breeds of dogs, and the dental disease appears to be related to the soft diets that these animals are fed.

How to keep your dog's teeth clean: Your Schnauzer's diet should meet not only its nutri-

tional requirements but also the physiologic needs of its teeth and jaws. A diet of crunchy dog biscuits or kibbled meal goes a long way in meeting this important function. Also, rawhide chew bones should be provided for your dog; not only do they help keep teeth and gums healthy, but they also give the dog a positive and socially acceptable way to spend part of its time (After all, your Schnauzer isn't *really* expected to work for its living, and because of this, it has time to get into trouble.)

How to clean your dog's teeth if already in need of care: Often, if your Schnauzer's teeth are only slightly covered with plaque or hard tartar, a chew bone may be sufficient to clean the teeth, but if you find a heavy accumulation of tartar, you can try one of the available canine toothpastes. Your veterinarian can aid you in selecting one. If, in the opinion of your veterinarian, your dog needs more aggressive dental hygiene, arrange for the professional cleaning that will make it easier to *keep* your pet's teeth clean.

Accustom your Schnauzer to routine home dental care as a puppy and your dog will benefit from enhanced health well into its senior years.

Today some of your dog's diseased teeth can be saved by appropriate endodontic therapy. Veterinary dentistry is developing rapidly and offers exciting opportunities for extending the life of your dog's teeth and general longevity.

Arthritis

As your Schnauzer ages, it may develop arthritis in one or more of its joints. Younger dog may acquire arthritic joints from bacterial infections or traumatic accidents, and these require the immediate care of a veterinarian. The most common age-related arthritis is called *osteoarthritis,* and it usually develops gradually over a period of months or years.

Prevention: The most effective way to prevent, or at least forestall osteoarthritis is to offer your Schnauzer adequate physical exercise. It is important that you not allow your pet to become obese, because each ounce of extra weight is an additional burden on its many joints. Making sure that your dog has a warm and draft-free place to sleep also may retard the development and pain of arthritis. Swimming is an excellent exercise for your pet's entire body.

Medical management: In the past, adrenal cortical steroid hormones and aspirin were the mainstays of veterinary medical management of canine arthritis. More recently, a group of "nonsteroidal anti-inflammatory" drugs have shown great promise in reducing joint inflammation and pain in dogs. Once a diagnosis of your dog's lameness is made, your veterinarian can prescribe one or more medications.

Are Dog Diseases Dangerous to Humans?

Obviously, rabies, bacterial infections arising out of dog-bite wounds, and exposure to infected urine from active cases of canine leptospirosis can be hazardous to humans, but there are few diseases that dogs and their owners share. Some fungal skin diseases such as ringworm and the mite infestation known as scabies or mange can be transmitted from dogs to people—and vice versa. Several worm and protozoan parasites also affect people, but routine hygiene greatly lessens exposure to these organisms. The most common viral diseases of dogs, such as canine distemper, infectious canine hepatitis, parainfluenza, parvoviral gastroenteritis, and coronaviral gastroenteritis are not transmissible to humans.

More to the point, there are probably as many cases on record of dogs contracting diseases from their owners as the reverse. A number of cases of canine tuberculosis have been traced to their infected owners, but these are not common today because tuberculosis is no longer an endemic disease in the United States. The canine mouth is not necessarily more populated by dangerous bacteria than is the human mouth.

Exercise for You and Your Dog

You and your Schnauzer will benefit greatly from routine exercise; the amount and type of this activity can be tailored to the tolerance of both of you for physical exercise. At the least, a brisk walk around the block will be mutually beneficial. A run in the park or a swim in a nearby lake in good weather will maintain your dog's muscle tone and psychological balance. As your dog ages, the amount of exertion should be adjusted to its abilities.

If you wish to trot your dog alongside as you bicycle, be certain to allow your pet's foot and toe pads to be accustomed to the extra wear by gradually increasing exposure to the pavement over a period of several weeks. In very warm or humid weather, allow your dog to rest at intervals so that it can dissipate its increased body temperature. Dogs do not have sweat glands distributed over their entire bodies and must rely upon panting to exhaust the bulk of excess heat. Ready access to fresh water also is a must.

A Veterinarian's View of Euthanasia: A Last Act of Love

Euthanasia, from the Greek *good + death:* painlessly inducing death, for reasons of mercy, of patients suffering from incurable disease or injury.

As a veterinary surgeon, I have always appreciated the enormous privilege of being able to end the suffering of some of my patients. We live at a time when it is possible to extend the life of many patients, but we always must be acutely aware that by doing so we also may be extending their exposure to intense and constant pain. In other words, too often attempts to prolong the life of a patient result only in prolonged dying. No humane person would knowingly subject another creature to suffering, but often during my professional career I have not been able to persuade an otherwise loving pet owner to finally "let go" and allow an animal companion to die and thus be released from a terribly painful existence. In many cases it was clear to me that the reason for this reluctance to part from an obviously suffering pet was based solely upon the owner's sense of impending loss, and little or no consideration was given to the plight of the animal.

The decision to permit euthanasia is a deeply personal one and can be made only after great emotional soul-searching. The caring veterinarian realizes that euthanasia is a terribly painful choice, and stands ready to be supportive when that decision must be made. Our profession can, if called upon, end our patients' suffering by acts of *commission;* our physician colleague must rely solely upon acts of *omission.* That difference is of immense importance and we do not consider it lightly.

Dealing with the Loss of a Much-Loved Pet

As a veterinarian engaged in clinical practice, the most difficult thing I must face is having to tell an owner that a pet either has died or will soon die. This situation has always been most heartfelt when the owner lived alone with the pet as an only companion.

To grieve over the loss of a loved one is absolutely normal, whether that loved one was a fellow human being or a pet animal.

Today there is increasing interest and research into the "human-animal bond" that exists between people and their pets. For some persons, a loved pet is an "anchor to reality" that for one or more reasons serves as a surrogate for human companionship.

If you are experiencing difficulty in deciding whether to allow your loved pet to die peacefully, refer to the list of professionals trained to help you in this time of personal loss. You may also wish to read *Companion Animal Loss and Pet Owner Grief* by Marc A. Rosenberg (ALPO Pet Center).

CHARACTERISTICS OF SCHNAUZERS

The following descriptions are based on the AKC standards. The text is given almost in full for the Miniature Schnauzer; only size and color are given for the Standard and Giant Schnauzers.

General appearance: The Miniature Schnauzer is a robust, active dog of terrier type, resembling his larger cousin, the Standard Schnauzer, in general appearance, and has an alert, active disposition. He is sturdily built, nearly square in proportion of body length to height, with plenty of bone, and without any suggestion of toyishness. The Giant Schnauzer should resemble, as nearly as possible, in general appearance, a larger and more powerful version of the Standard Schnauzer.

Temperament: The typical Miniature Schnauzer is alert and spirited, yet obedient to command. He is friendly, intelligent, and willing to please. He should never be over-aggressive or timid.

Head: Strong and rectangular, its width diminishing slightly from ears to eyes, and again to tip of nose. Forehead unwrinkled. Topskull flat and fairly long. Foreface parallel to topskull, with

All the Schnauzers share a robust nature, handsome appearance and lots of brain power. It comes as no surprise that these wonderful dogs have been so well-loved for so long.

a slight stop, and is at least as long as topskull. Muzzle strong in proportion to skull; it ends in a moderately blunt manner, with thick whiskers which accentuate rectangular shape of head. *Teeth:* Meet in a scissors bite, that is, upper front teeth overlap lower front teeth in such a manner that inner surface of upper incisors barely touches outer surface of lower incisors when mouth is closed. *Eyes:* Small, dark brown, and deep-set; oval in appearance and keen in expression. *Ears:* When cropped, ears identical in shape and length, with pointed tips; in balance with head and not exaggerated in length; set high on skull and carried perpendicularly at inner edges, with as little bell as possible along outer edges. When uncropped, ears are small and V-shaped, folding close to skull.

Neck: Strong and well arched, blending into shoulders, and with skin fitting tightly at throat.

Body: Short and deep, with brisket extending at least to elbows. Ribs well sprung and deep, extending well back to a short loin. Underbody does not present a tucked-up appearance at flank. Topline is straight; it declines slightly from withers to base of tail. Overall length from chest to stern bone appears to equal height at withers.

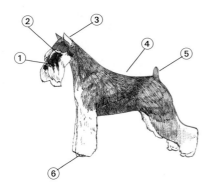

Miniature Schnauzer Illustrated Standard

1. Head strong, rectangular, and long
2. Eyes small, oval, and deep set
3. Ears set high; carried erect and pointed if cropped; if uncropped, small and V-shaped, folding close to the skull
4. Topline straight, slopes slightly down
5. Tail set high and carried erect, docked just long enough to be visible over backline
6. Cat feet

❑ **Color:** salt and pepper, black and silver, or black
❑ **DQ:** under 12" or over 14", white except for small white spot permitted on chest of black dogs (white not to be confused with silver white under throat and chest)

Forequarters: Have flat, somewhat sloping shoulders and high withers. Forelegs straight and parallel when viewed from all sides; strong pasterns and good bone; separated by a fairly deep brisket which precludes a pinched front. Elbows close, and ribs spread gradually from first rib so as to allow space for elbows to move close to body.

Hindquarters: Have strong-muscled, slanting thighs; well bent at stifles and straight from hock to so-called heel; sufficient angulation so that, in stance, hocks extend beyond tail. Hindquarters never appear overbuilt or higher than the shoulders.

Feet: Short and round (cat feet) with thick, black pads. Toes arched and compact.

Movement: The trot is the gait at which movement is judged. When approaching, forelegs, with elbows close to body, move straight forward, neither too close not too far apart. Going away, hind legs are straight and travel in same planes as forelegs. *Note: It is generally accepted that when a full trot is achieved, rear legs continue to move in same planes as forelegs, but a very slight inward inclination will occur. It begins at point of shoulder in front and at hip joint in rear. Viewed from front or rear, legs are straight from these points to pads. Degree of inward inclination is almost imperceptible in a Miniature Schnauzer that has correct movement. It does not justify moving close, toeing in, crossing, or moving out at elbows. Viewed from side, forelegs have good reach, while hind legs have strong drive, with good pick-up of hocks. Feet turn neither inward nor outward.*

Tail: Set high and carried erect. Docked only long enough to be clearly visible over topline of body when dog is in proper length of coat.

Coat: Double, with hard, wiry outer coat and close undercoat. Head, neck, and body coat must be plucked. When in show condition body coat should be of sufficient length to determine texture. Close covering on neck, ears, and skull. Furnishings fairly thick but not silky.

Size: From 12 to 14 inches (30.7–35.8 cm). ideal size 13½ inches (34.6 cm).

Color: Recognized colors are salt and pepper, black and silver, and solid black. Typical color is salt and pepper in shades of gray; tan shading is permissible. Salt-and-pepper mixture fades out to light gray or silver white in eyebrows,

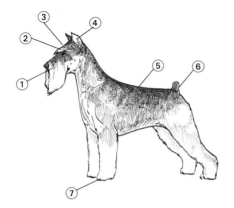

Standard Schnauzer Illustrated Standard

(1) Expression alert and spirited
(2) Eyes oval with long eyebrows, which should not impair vision
(3) Head strong, rectangular, and long
(4) Ears set high; carried erect if cropped; V-shaped and mobile so they break at skull level if uncropped
(5) Topline slopes slightly down
(6) Tail carried erect and docked from 1 to 2"
(7) Feet small, round, compact

❏ **Color:** pepper and salt or pure black
❏ **DQ:** males under 18" or over 20"; females under 17" or over 19"

whiskers, cheeks, under throat, across chest, under tail, leg furnishings, under body, and inside legs. Light underbody hair not to rise higher on sides of body than front elbows.

Black and silvers follow same pattern as salt and peppers. Entire salt-and-pepper section must be black.

Black the only solid color allowed. Must be a true black with no gray hairs and no brown tinge except where whiskers may have become discolored. Small white spot on chest permitted.

The Standard Schnauzer

Size: Ideal height at highest point of shoulder blades, 18½ to 19½ inches (47.4–50 cm) for males and 17½ to 18½ (44.8–47.4 cm) for females.

Color: Pepper and salt; pure black.

The Giant Schnauzer

Size: The height of the withers is 25½ to 27½ inches (65.3–70.5 cm) for males and 23½ to 25½ inches (60.2–65.3 cm) for females.

Color: Solid black or pepper and salt.

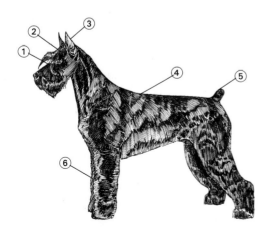

Giant Schnauzer Illustrated Standard

(1) Rectangular head
(2) Oval deep-set eyes
(3) Ears may be cropped or uncropped; when uncropped, ears are V-shaped
(4) Short, straight back
(5) Tail docked to second or third joint, carried high
(6) Cat feet

❏ **Color:** solid black or pepper and salt
❏ **DQ:** overshot or undershot, markings other than specified

INFORMATION

Kennel and Breed Clubs

American Kennel Club (AKC) Registrations
5580 Centerview Drive
Raleigh, NC 27606-3390
(919) 233-9767
Website: www.akc.org

The Canadian Kennel Club
89 Skyway Avenue, Suite 100
Etobicoke, Ontario, Canada
M9W6R4
(416) 675-5511

Federation Cynologique Internationale
Secretariat General de la FCA
Place Albert 1er, 13
B-6530 Thuin, Belgium
Website: www.fci.be/english

The Kennel Club
1-4 Clarages Street, Picadilly
London W7Y 8AB England

   The American Miniature Schnauzer Club,
The Giant Schnauzer Club of America, and The
Standard Schnauzer Club of America are
the parent clubs for the breeds in the United
States. The names and addresses for their
current Secretaries may be accessed through
the American Kennel Club as listed above.

United Kennel Club (UKC)
100 East Kilgore Road
Kalamazoo, MI 49001-5598
(616) 343-9020

United States Dog Agility Association
P.O. Box 850955
Richardson, TX 75085-8955

(972) 231-9700
Fax: (214) 503-0161
Website: www.usdaa.com
E-mail: info@usdaa.com

Health Related Associations and Foundations

American Society for the Prevention of Cruelty
   to Animals (ASPCA)
424 East 92nd Street
New York, NY 10128-6804
(212) 876-7700
Website: www.aspca.org

American Veterinary Medical Association (AVMA)
930 North Meacham Road
Schaumburg, IL 60173
Website: www.avma.org

Canine Eye Registration Foundation (CERF)
South Campus Court, Building C
West Lafayette, IN 47907

National Animal Poison Control Center (NAPCC)
Animal Product Safety Service
1717 South Philo Road, Suite 36
Urbana, IL 61802
(888) 4ANI-HELP
(888) 426-4435
(900) 680-0000
(Consultation fees apply; call for details.)
Website: www.napcc.aspca.org

Orthopedic Foundation for Animals (OFA)
2300 Nifong Boulevard
Columbia, MO 65201
Website: www.prodogs.com

Therapy Dogs International
P.O. Box 2796
Cheyenne, WY 82203

Lost Pet Registries

The American Kennel Club (AKC)
AKC Companion Recovery
5580 Centerview Drive, Suite 250
Raleigh, NC 27606-3394
(800) 252-7894
Website: www.akc.org/car.htm
E-mail: found@akc.org

Home Again Microchip Service
(800) LONELY-ONE

National Dog Registry (NDR)
P.O. Box 118
Woodstock, NY 12498-0116
(800) 637-3647

Petfinders
368 High Street
Athol, NY 12810
(800) 223-4747

Tattoo-A-Pet
1625 Emmons Avenue
Brooklyn, NY 11235
(800) TATTOOS

Periodicals

The American Kennel Club Gazette
260 Madison Avenue
New York, NY 10016

Dog Fancy
Subscription Division
P.O. Box 53264
Boulder, CO 80323-3264
(303) 786-7306/666-8504
Website: www.dogfancy.com

Dogs USA Annual
P.O. Box 55811
Boulder, CO 80322-5811
(303) 786-7652

Dog World
260 Madison Avenue
New York, NY 10016

Books

The Complete Dog Book. Official Publication of the American Kennel Club. New York: Howell Book House, 1997.

Coile, D. Caroline. *Encyclopedia of Dog Breeds*. Hauppauge, NY: Barron's Educational Series, Inc., 1998.

___. *Show Me! A Dog Show Primer*. Hauppauge, NY: Barron's Educational Series, Inc., 1997.

Dille, Barbara M. *Standard Schnauzer: A Complete and Reliable Handbook*. Neptune City, New Jersey: TFH Publications, 1997.

Gallant, Johan. *The World of Schnauzers: Standard, Giant and Miniature*. Loveland, Colorado: Alpine Publications/Best Friends, Ltd., 1996.

Kiedrowski, Dan. *The New Miniature Schnauzer: The Breed Since Ch. Dorem Display*, 2nd ed. New York: Howell Book House, 1997.

Pryor, Karen. *Don't Shoot the Dog! The New Art of Teaching and Training*. New York: Bantam, Doubleday, Dell, 1999.

Siegal, Mordecai, and University of California-Davis, School of Veterinary Medicine Faculty and Staff. *UC Davis Book of Dogs: A Complete Medical Reference Guide for Dogs & Puppies*. New York: HarperCollins, 1995.

About the Author

Dr. Fredric L. Frye was a clinical professor of medicine at the University of California's School of Veterinary Medicine, Davis, for over 26 years. A recipient of the Practitioner's Research Award of the American Veterinary Medical Association, he is the author of over 350 papers and articles dealing with dogs, cats, large domestic animals, reptiles, amphibians, and invertebrates, among other subjects. His more than 20 books include *First Aid for Your Dog* (Barron's); *First Aid for Your Cat* (Barron's); *Mutts* (Barron's); *Husbandry, Medicine and Surgery of Captive Reptiles; Phyllis, Phallus, Genghis Cohen and Other Creatures I Have Known; A Practical Guide to Feeding Captive Reptiles; A Guide to Successful Management of Captive Invertebrates; The Reptile Clinician's Handbook; Iguana iguana;* and *Veterinary Comparative Histology.* He is now engaged in cancer research and teaching.

Photo Credits

Pets by Paulette: pages 3, 5, 9, 16 bottom, 17, 24, 25, 28 bottom right, 29 top, 40, 48, 49 top left, 49 bottom, 53, 64, 77, 84, 93; Kent and Donna Dannen: pages 8, 13, 16 top, 28 top left, 28 top right, 28 bottom left, 29 bottom left, 29 bottom right, 32, 33, 36, 37, 45, 56, 57, 60, 61, 68, 69, 80, 85, 88, 89; Tara Darling; pages 4, 12, 20, 21, 41, 44, 49 top right, 52, 65.

Important Note

This book is concerned with buying, keeping, and raising Schnauzers. The publisher and the author think it is important to point out that the advice and information for Schnauzer maintenance applies to healthy, normally developed animals. Anyone who buys an adult Schnauzer or one from an animal shelter must consider that the animal may have behavioral problems and may, for example, bite without any visible provocation. Such anxiety-biters are dangerous for the owner as well as for the general public.

Caution is further advised in the association of children with a Schnauzer, in meetings with other dogs, and in exercising the dog without a leash.

Dedication

To Brucye, Lorraine, and Erik, and to Raisin, who first introduced us to the joys of Schnauzer companionship.

Cover Photos

Front Cover: Kent and Donna Dannen; Back Cover: Pets by Paulette; Inside Front Cover: Kent and Donna Dannen; Inside Back Cover: Kent and Donna Dannen.

All inquiries should be addressed to:
Barron's Educational Series, Inc.
250 Wireless Boulevard
Hauppauge, NY 11788
http://www.barronseduc.com

ISBN-13: 978-0-7641-1962-0
ISBN-10: 0-7641-1962-1

Library of Congress Catalog Card No. 2001043296

Library of Congress Cataloging-in-Publication Data
Frye, Fredric L.
    Schnauzers : everything about purchase, care, nutrition, and diseases : with a special chapter on understanding schnauzers / Fredric L. Frye.
    p. cm. (A complete pet owner's manual)
Includes bibliographical references (p.). and index.
ISBN 0-7641-1962-1 (alk. paper)
1. Schnauzers. I. Title. II. Series.
SF429.S37 F78 2002
636.73—dc21   2001043296

Printed in China
19 18 17 16 15 14 13 12 11